# WITTGENSTEIN AND METAPHOR

## Jerry H. Gill

UNIVERSITY
PRESS OF
AMERICA

FOR

PETER GENCO

"A Person for Others"

--Table of Contents--

WITTGENSTEIN AND METAPHOR

by Jerry H. Gill

# Introduction

This book represents an initial attempt to
do something about a significant philosophical
anomaly. In spite of the fact that Wittgenstein's writings are absolutely replete with
metaphor--and in spite of the fact that he is
the only so-called "analytic" philosopher to
write in this manner-there exist no treatments
of his use and/or theory of metaphor. In pur-
suing this oddity I have come to the conclusion
that there is an important relationship between
the metaphoric quality of Wittgenstein's writings and his conception of philosophy. In a
word, I am convinced that Wittgenstein views
philosophy as an essentially metaphoric activity. Thus his unique style not only _befits_
his approach, it is the _fulcrum_ from which his
philosophic explorations achieve their force.

In Part One I present a survey of the
main current views of the nature of metaphor,
both to provide a backdrop against which to
appreciate Wittgenstein's use of this mode of
speech and to develop insights which can be
helpful in coming to grips with the notion of
metaphor nascent within that use. I begin with
a discussions of two relatively popular, yet
seemingly opposed points of view, those of
Paul Tillich and Paul Edwards. The former
thinks of metaphorical speech, expecially
theological uses of it, as symbolic and essentially irreducible to other modes of discourse.
The latter defines metaphor as either "translatable" into literal, factual speech or nonsensical. I next move to a brief appraisal of
the position developed by Suzanne Langer, which
for all strong points remains essentially dualistic and "positivistic" in orientation. Chapter One concludes with a brief consideration
of Colin Turbayne's view that although we must
make use of metaphoric speech, it is important

to remember that it is _only_ metaphor and not factually true.

Next, the more sophisticated, as well as more helpful, views of Philip Wheelwright, Monroe Beardsley, and Walker Percy are considered. They view metaphoric speech as effecting an interaction between two realms of discourse customarily unrelated to one another. When successful this interaction evokes a heightened understanding of both of the dimensions of experience involved, but primarily of one by means of the other. All of these thinkers, each in his own way, contend that this increased understanding is cognitive in character and thus metaphoric speech is neither _sui generis_, as with Tillich and Langer, nor reducible to literal speech, as with Edwards. Moreover, I suggest that both would view Turbayne's warning concerning the "misleading" character of metaphoric thought and language as misplaced, since it implies that this mode of understanding is somehow inferior to some other when in fact it is indispensable.

In Chapter Three I take up the even more far-reaching and helpful views of Nelson Goodman, Paul Ricoeur, and certain other writers such as Hans-Georg Gadamer and Owen Barfield. These thinkers, in addition to stressing the evocative role of metaphoric speech, emphasize what I call the "constitutive" function of metaphor as well. That is, they maintain that at the deepest level all thought and speech are rooted in awarenesses and reasonings which, while serving as the basis for more explicit forms of knowledge and language, can only be expressed by means of the metaphoric mode. In a word, the metaphors in which these insights are expressed constitute the very framework within which other modes of thought and expression can and do take place.

In Part Two I seek to identify and expli-
cate briefly the main and obvious metaphors employed by Wittgenstein in three of his major
works: Tractatus Logic-Philosophicus (Chapter
Four), Philosophical Investigations (Chapter
Five), and On Certainty (Chapter Six). The purpose of these chapters is to provide the "spade
work: for Part Three, not to expound on the
meaning of Wittgenstein's individual metaphors.
Although ultimately the two blend into one another, the focus of this book is not on the content of Wittgenstein's philosophic explorations,
but rather on the significance of his manner of
treatment of the issues with which he deals.

Perhaps it should be pointed out that I
provide no clear-cut definition of what constitutes a metaphor, whether in general or for
Wittgenstein in particular. There are three
reasons for this. One is simply that most discussions of the nature of metaphor do not so
begin, perhaps because such a definition is what
they are aiming toward, not what they are starting from. Secondly, and this may in part explain
the above phenomenon, most people recognize a
metaphor when confronted with one; generally we
can distinguish between them and so-called
"literal" speech. There are borderline cases,
to be sure, but these are more the exception
than the rule. Thirdly, it is in keeping with
the above observation and with Wittgenstein's
own approach to meaning to begin not with definitions but with usage.

Also, it should be acknowledged that in
one sense, but only in one sense, the material
presented and discussed in Part Two is quite
familiar, and in no way advances our understanding of Wittgenstein's thought. The main contention of this entire study is that scholars working with Wittgenstein's philosophy have become
so familiar with his mode, while attending to
his meaning, that they have failed to notice,

let alone grasp, the significance of the
former for the latter.  Here is an important
and obvious case in which "the medium is the
message", and yet there exist no explorations
of the use and meaning of metaphor in Wittgenstein's writings.  So in one sense it is all
too familiar; but in another and important
sense it remains painfully unfamiliar.  I submit that a simple consideration of the main
metaphors in Wittgenstein's major works, together with the significance thereof, is essentially unexplored and exceedingly rich territory.

It is in Part Three that all of the above
is, hopefully, brought to fruition.  For here I
try to develop an overall view of Wittgenstein's
"theory" of metaphor, based on his use of this
mode of speech in conjunction with his insights
concerning language and philosophy.  It is
acknowledged at the outset that Wittgenstein
offered no explicit theory of metaphor.  Nevertheless, he seems to have found it impossible
to think and write without prolific use of them.
Indeed, it could be argued that no philosopher
in Western history ever made such extensive use
of this mode of thought and expression.  Moreover, it is my contention that it is precisely
here that the revolutionary and profound character of Wittgenstein's approach is to be
found.

Chapter Seven begins with a brief summary
of Part Two and subsequent placing of Wittgenstein's metaphoric usage in relation to the
various views surveyed in Part One.  It then
moves to a broader consideration of the later
Wittgenstein's theory of language and meaning,
with special attention being given to the harmony between this and his own use of metaphor.
The focus here is on meaning as a function of
use, based in overlapping and "imprecise" and
"incomplete" language-games.  Chapter Eight
takes up the issue of the cognitive status of
the metaphoric mode.  I first develop a correlation between Wittgenstein's epistemological

insights in On Certainty and Michael Polanyi's distinction between explicit and tacit knowledge. Then I seek to show that it is precisely the constitutive function of metaphor that is appropriate to Wittgenstein's, as well as Polanyi's, epistemological position -- and that Wittgenstein himself uses metaphors in this manner.

The final chapter shifts to a consideration of Wittgenstein's view of philosophy, as "conceptual therapy", as distinguished from both the traditional "super-science" and positivist "verificationist" interpretations. I argue that for Wittgenstein philosophical problems are neither solved nor dissolved, but are rather "resolved", by means of returning to the natural home of speech, namely everyday experience and ordinary language. My concluding claim is that central to this therapy, or resolvement, is the notion of metaphor; that in Wittgenstein's view philosophical muddles arise when we try to "escape" or eliminate metaphor, and that the way out of such muddles is to "invite" participation in metaphoric discourse as a way of seeing things afresh. Correlations are drawn between Wittgenstein's view of philosophy and those of John Wisdom and Alan Pasch. In short, for Wittgenstein philosophy is a metaphoric activity.

This, then, is the plan and the purpose. It should be emphasized that this is an initial exploration. Nevertheless, it is both an important venture and hopefully, a stimulating one.

# Chapter One

## -- Metaphor As Symbol Or Substitute --

By way of providing a general backdrop
against which more readily and clearly to
appreciate Wittgenstein's use of metaphor, it
will prove helpful to begin with a survey of
various notions of the nature and logic of
metaphoric language as developed by important
representative thinkers.  In addition, such a
survey will afford useful insights for the development of the overall, if implicit, understanding of metaphor embodied in Wittgenstein's use thereof.  Such are the broad purposes of Part One.

More specifically, in this first chapter
the aim is to introduce the standard dichotomy
that is often drawn between symbolic or figurative expression on the one hand and literal
or factual language on the other.  This dualistic interpretation is taken to be the least
helpful approach to the task of understanding
metaphor, and thus represents a kind of "ground
zero" for our overall exploration.  I shall begin with a brief discussion of the rather simplistic postures of the existentialist thinker
Paul Tillich and the positivist thinker Paul
Edwards.  Then the highly sophisticated and
influential dualism of Suzanne Langer will be
taken up, followed by an examination of Colin
Turbayne's subtle yet flawed critique of the
metaphoric mode, per se.

### 1.   Paul Tillich and Paul Edwards

In the section of his Systematic Theology
entitled "The Reality of God", Tillich discusses such questions as the existence and nature

1

of God. After defining God as "the ground" and "structure" of "Being-itself", Tillich takes up the possibility of knowledge of God as so defined. This, in turn, raises the problem of the meaning of religious language, or God-talk. He wastes no time in clearly stating his position: "The statement that God is being-itself is a non-symbolic statement. It does not point beyond itself. It means what it says directly and properly. However, after this has been said, nothing else can be said about God as God which is not symbolic." [1]

This position, that all language about God (except the statement 'God is being-itself') is symbolic, is based on a fundamental distinction between 'sign' and 'symbol'. A sign, for Tillich, has an arbitrary relation to that to which it points (e.g. a table could be designated by a sign other than 'table', if people were so to stipulate), while a symbol "participates in the reality for which it stands." [2] The term 'God' is said to "participate in the power of the divine to which it points," [3] rather than designate one being among others within the totality of reality.

In response to the question of how a symbol derived from finite experience can function as a symbol of that which is infinite, Tillich maintains that only when God is viewed as being-itself can the concept of God-talk as analogical be accepted. If God is viewed as another being among beings, then it is impossible to bridge the gap between the finite and the infinite. However, if God is conceived of as being-itself then all statements about the finite become statements about the infinite, and vice versa. [4]

In his Dynamics of Faith, which came seven years after the first volume of Systematic Theology, Tillich hedges a bit on the question of the non-symbolic nature of the statement "God is being-itself." As the result of an early criticism of his view of God-talk as exclusively symbolic in nature, Tillich had taken the position in his Systematic Theology that the statement that God is being-itself is the only possible and necessary non-symbolic statement about God. This single, non-symbolic statement was seen as necessary in order to insure the ultimate objective referent of all God-talk. When, however, he discusses,"The Symbols of Faith" in Dynamics of Faith, Tillich fails to say anything about the possibility, or necessity, of a non-symbolic statement about God.

> Whatever we say about that which concerns us ultimately, whether or not we call it God, has a symbolic meaning. It points beyond itself while participating in that to which it points. In no other way can faith express itself adequately. The language of faith is the language of symbols. If faith were what we have shown that it is not, such an assertion could not be made. But faith, understood as the state of being ultimately concerned, has no language other than symbols. When saying this I always expect the question: Only a symbol? He who asks this question shows that he has not understood the difference between sign and symbols nor the power of symbolic language, which surpasses in quality and strength the power of any nonsymbolic language.[5]

It cannot be denied that in this passage Tillich seems to negate his earlier position on the non-symbolic nature of the statement 'God is being-itself.' One could perhaps maintain that since Dynamics of Faith was written on a more popular level, Tillich did not want to bring up such a technical matter. In view of the importance of this issue, however, such an

3

argument appears a bit weak.  As near as I am
able to determine, his final statement of his
position is found in a symposium of "Religious
Experience and Truth".  There Tillich said:

> But the word 'God' involves a double
> meaning: it connotes the unconditioned
> transcendent, the ultimate, and also an
> object somehow endowed with qualities
> and actions.  The first is not figura-
> tive or symbolic but is rather in the
> strictist sense what it is said to be.
> The second, however, is really, sym-
> bolic, figurative. [6]

Here he reiterates his original position, maintaining that the statement about God as being-
itself is non-symbolic, while all other descriptions about him are symbolic.

There are two chief difficulties with
Tillich's understanding of figurative language
which render it unfruitful as a theory of metaphor.  First, it is not developed in anything
like a systematic or thorough fashion.  We
would need a much wider application and set of
examples illustrating the differences between
signs and symbols in order to fully understand
and evaluate his position.  Second, on the basis
of what we do have it must be concluded that his
distinction is far too simplistic to do justice
either to the notion of sign or to the notion
of symbol.  Not only do symbols often become
sign and vice versa: but both signs and symbols are far more complex than Tillich's definitions would allow.  For one thing, personal
names would seem to function both as symbols
and as signs.  For another, symbols (and metaphors) often have a stronger connection with factual considerations than Tillich seems to think.
To use his example, some flags look somewhat
alike and it would be important to settle which
one was involved when determining a question of

patriotism and/or treason. Moreover, the possibility that symbolic or metaphoric speech could function on more than one level simultaneously never seems to occur to Tillich. As we shall see, this notion of polisignification is crucial to the logic of metaphor.

At the opposite extreme is the position of Paul Edwards, which may be thought of as a kind of over-reaction to the abstract and diffuse theory offered by Tillich. In fact, Edwards' view (and its confusions) is pointedly focused in an article of his entitled "Professor Tillich's Confusions". [7] A brief examination of his position will make evident its diametric opposition to that of Tillich as well as its own inherent inadequacies.

To begin at the heart of the matter, Edwards' conception of language is essentially "reductionistic". By this I mean that he maintains a sharp distinction between the cognitive function of language and other functions such as emotive, imperative, et. al. More specifically, he insists that unless a statement is "reducible" to a "literal equivalent" it is "devoid of cognitive meaning". In this particular article, Edwards' explicit concern is with the reducibility of metaphorical language, and the following quotation makes his position extremely clear:

But we know this (what common metaphors mean) because we can eliminate the metaphorical expression, because we can specify the content of the assertion in non-metaphorical language, because we can supply the literal equivalent... in calling a metaphor 'reducible' all I mean is that the truth-claims made by the sentence in which it occurs can be reproduced by one or more sentences contains an irreducible metaphor, it follows at once that the sentence is devoid of cognitive meaning, that

5

it is unintelligible, that it fails to
make a genuine assertion.

Speaking generally, Edwards presents his
arguments in such a way as to appear completely
oblivious of the difficulties inherent in a view
of language which necessitates a sharp dichotomy between the cognitive and noncognitive uses
of language. Moreover, the implications of such
terms as 'reducibility' and 'literal' point up
the similarity of Edwards' view to that of "logical atomism" and the "picture theory of language". The work of the later Wittgenstein,
J.L. Austin and Gilbert Ryle has been aimed
specifically at undermining this reductionistic
view of language--and with a good deal of success!
Simply naming certain important philosophers who
disagree with his assumptions does not score
"philosophical points" against Edwards, but pointing out his seeming lack of awareness of the work
of such thinkers does.

Nowhere is Edwards' confusion more evident
than in his use of the term 'literal'. Not only
does he fail to offer any definition of this
term, he proceeds as if he were completely unaware that there are serious difficulties connected with it. Certain statements of Edward's
would indicate that by 'literal' he means designating "features" of reality which can be "observed". Without dragging out all the standard
difficulties relating to the term 'observe', it
is enough to suggest that Edwards sharpen his
key term before he builds his case on it, if in
fact his position is that precision is a necessary condition for meaningfulness.

It is apparent that Edwards operates with
an understanding of the nature of metaphor which
is far too narrow. First off, he is mistaken
about how it is that metaphorical expressions
are used and understood in everyday discourse.

6

The passage quoted above makes it clear that Edwards maintains that we understand ("know the meaning of") common metaphors because we can reduce them to literal statements. Not only is it not true that people learn to use and understand metaphors by "projecting from", and "reducing to", certain statements about observable features, it is decidedly not the case that people who use and understand metaphors can supply the "literal equivalent" when called upon to do so. In ordinary discourse involving metaphors, one uses and understands them without giving the slightest thought to how they ought to be, or might be, so reduced.

The most ironic thing about Edwards' presentation is his failure to realize that even his own statements make use of metaphorical phrases for which he would be hard put to provide a "literal equivalent". This is just another way of saying that Edwards does not seem to be aware of the fact that ordinary speech is "shot through" with metaphor. On his view, all language is built upon, and reducible to, language about the "observable features" (or perhaps sensedate?) of experience. The similarities between Edwards' view and that of those who have sought, without success, to construct an "ideal language" are obvious. To maintain that the metaphorical use of language is derivative from language about "observable features: is to betray a shallow, if not upside down, understanding of language.

Throughout his article, Edwards uses such terms as: 'in', 'sense', 'follows', 'turning', 'posses', 'point', and 'see'. Most often he is not using these terms in what could be called an "observable feature" sense, but since such uses are part of the weave of ordinary language one would

7

hesitate to call these uses metaphorical.
I doubt very much whether Edwards was aware
of the complexity of the seemingly incidental terms which he used to present his argument, let alone that he would be able to reduce his entire presentation to "literal"
statements. My point is simply that the
metaphorical use of language cannot be so
easily separated from the rest of human discourse without threatening the framework of
language itself.

Strangely, Edwards avoids mentioning
the difficulties raised for his view by the
close logical connection between metaphors
and the models used in the physical and social
sciences. It is not a secret that the "reducibility view" of language has long since become inadequate when dealing with the complex
constructs of science. The importance of
analogue computers is just one case in point.
The concepts of "electron particle", "elec-
tro-magnetic field", "historical cause,"
"defense mechanism", and "cultural lag" are
all metaphorical in a sense. Yet, it is often difficult to reduce or eliminate such
concepts without falling back (metaphorically!) on other terms and phrases which are
equally far removed from "literal equivalents."
Clearly, we shall have to look elsewhere for
more helpful notions of metaphor.

## 2. Susanne Langer

In the wake of logical empiricism, with
its emotivist interpretation of aesthetic expression, the work of Susanne K. Langer seems
to provide a powerful and comprehensive alternative view. Whereas meanings had been limited, by such thinkers as Paul Edwards, to logical and empirical discourse, Langer seeks to

make a solid case for a parallel system of meaning within artistic expression. Her dualistic approach carries important implications for a theory of metaphor, implications we shall confront shortly. Incidentally, while Ms. Langer's view is similar to Tillich's in that it is dualistic, it will soon be apparent that hers is far more comprehensive.

It is my contention that Langer's alternative view fails to strike deep enough to undercut the root of the logical empiricist criterion of meaning. Her move is to accept this criterion for discursive expression (language proper) while offering a separate but parallel interpretation of meaning for artistic, including metaphorical, expression. What is needed, however, is a thorough uprooting of the logical empiricist understanding of language in general so as to expose its deep inadequacy. When linguistic meaning is thus liberated one is free to explore the relation between language and art without either the pressure to reduce one to the other or the necessity to insist that they are totally distinct. More specifically, it no longer remains necessary to classify metaphoric meaning as either one or the other.

In source and goal Langer sees art and language as essentially the same. Both flow out of human consciousness and the impulse to symbolic expression or articulation. Moreover, both flow toward abstraction and depth of understanding. In their means of articulation and form of abstract understanding, however, art and language are seen by Langer as fundamentally different. While it is this contrast which most powerfully characterizes Langer's point of view, it should always be understood as a contrast which exists within

9

the broader context of similarity of source and goal. It is this dual similarity which accounts for the ever-arching parallelism between art and language in Langer's position. Art and language are not just different, they are different ways of doing the same thing.

Arising out of a common source--human consciousness-art and language part company immediately. According to Langer, artistic expression gives symbolic articulation to the "inner life", while language articulates our "outer life". Our consciousness of our subjective experience gives rise to feelings which express themselves artistically and our consciousness of our interaction with the world around us--outer experience--gives rise to thoughts and beliefs which express themselves linguistically. Furthermore, feeling as well as thought seeks abstract understanding. But there are differences here also. For while the sort of understanding that results from linguistic activity is general and conceptual in nature, that which results from artistic activity is concrete and perceptual. Both, however, aim at insight and are grounded in intuition. In their abstractness they differ as well. The conceptual abstractness of linguistic expression takes the form of generalization, while the perceptual abstractness of expression always takes a concrete or specific form.

> "But the abstractive process of art
> is entirely different from that of
> science, mathematics, and logic; just
> as the forms abstracted in art are not
> those of rational discourse, which serve
> us to symbolize public 'fact,' but com-
> plex forms capable of symbolizing the
> dynamics of subjective experience, the
> pattern of vitality, sentience, feel-
> ing, and emotion. Such forms cannot

10

be revealed by means of progressive
generalization; this makes the whole
development of art and all its techniques radically different from those
of discursive thought. Although art
and science spring from the same root,
namely, the impulse to symbolic expres-
sion--or which the richest, strongest,
and undoubtedly oldest manifestation
is language--they separate practically
from the beginning.
    A work of art is and remains
specific."[8]

Now for a closer look at Langer's contrast between language and art. She views
language as essentially representational in
character. Words are names and combinations
of words refer to states of affairs in our
outer life. In parallel fashion, she views
artistic expression as essentially presentational in nature. It presents the content
and structure of our inner life.

"Yet subjective existence has a structure; it is not only met from moment to
moment, but can be conceptually known,
reflected on, imagined and symbolically
expressed in detail and to a great depth.
Only it is not our usual medium, dis-
course--communication by language--
that serves to express what we know of
the life of feeling. There are logical
reasons why language fails to meet this
purpose, reasons I will not try to explain now. The important fact is that
what language does not readily do--pre-
sent the nature and patterns of sensi-
tive and emotional life--is done by
works of art. Such works are expressive forms, and what they express is
the nature of human feeling."[9]

11

There are three main aspects of Langer's crucial contrast between artistic expression as presentational and linguistic expression as representational. First, she contends that art presents the "felt life" <u>directly</u>, while language represents outer life <u>indirectly</u>. Secondly, artistic presentation is embodied in expressive form while linguistic representation is embodied in discursive form. Third, although art and language are both symbolic activities, the former is <u>iconic</u> while the latter is <u>non-iconic</u>. The principles of formulation in artistic presentation involve the construction of an apparition which is itself the locus of import.

> "The word is just an instrument. Its meaning lies elsewhere, and once we have grasped its connotation or identified something as its denotation we do not need the word any more. But a work of art does not point us to a meaning beyond its own presence. What is expressed cannot be grasped apart from the sensuous or poetic form that expresses it. In a work of art we have the direct presentation of a feeling, not a sign that points to it."[10]

There are two areas of special interest in Langer's position on the specific relation between art and language. One is the nature of <u>poetry</u>, which may be defined as the artistic use of language. Drawing a rather sharp distinction between "communication" (the purpose of discursive uses of language) and "formulation" (the goal of artistic endeavor), Langer places poetry in the latter classification.

> "Language is the material of poetry, but what is done with this material is not what we do with language in

actual life; for <u>poetry</u> <u>is</u> <u>not</u> <u>a</u> <u>kind</u>
<u>of</u> <u>discourse</u> <u>at</u> <u>all</u>. What the poet
creates out of words is an appearance
of events, persons, emotional reactions,
expressions, places, conditions of life;
these created things are the elements of
poetry; they constitute what Cecil Day
Lewis has called 'the poetic image.' A
poem is, in precisely his sense, an
image. This image is not necessarily
visual; since the word 'image' has an
almost irresistible connotation of visual-
ness, I prefer to call the poetic image
a <u>semblence</u>. The created poetic semblance need not be a semblance of corresponding actual things, facts, persons, or
experiences. It is quite normally a pure
appearance, a sheer figment; it is essentially a virtual object; and such a virtual object is a work of art. It is entirely created. Its material is language, its motif, or model, usually discursive speech, but what is created is
not actual discourse--what is created is
a composed and shaped apparition of a
new human experience."[11]

Proceeding to the implications of such a
view of the poetic use of language, Langer
discusses the relationship between the utterances of poetry and entities in the world to
which these utterances seem to refer. She
maintains that the real entities simulated in
a painting, sculpture, or piece of music are
only symbols used by the artist in his or her
effort to formulate an expressive form. The
simulations neither "represent" the entities
nor "symbolize" the meaning of the work of
art. It is its own meaning.

The second area of special interest, and for present purposes a more important one, is Langer's view of the role of metaphor. As would be expected, Langer conceives of metaphors as the vehicle for transforming the impulse to articulate inner experience into concrete, expressive form. Metaphor is the key to presenting "felt life" in artistic formulation so as to convey its meaning to the understanding directly.

"Whatever resists projection into the discursive form of language is, indeed, hard to hold in conception, and perhaps impossible to communicate, in the proper and strict sense of the word "communicate." But fortunately our logical intuition, or form-perception, is really much more powerful than we commonly believe, and our knowledge-- genuine knowledge, understanding--is considerably wider than our discourse. The principle of metaphor is simply the principle of saying one thing and meaning another, and expecting to be understood to mean the other. A metaphor is not language, it is an idea expressed by language, an idea that in its turn functions as a symbol to express something. It is not discursive and therefore does not really make a statement of the idea it conveys; but it formulates a new conception for our direct imaginative grasp."[12]

Somewhat unexpectedly, Langer also maintains that metaphor is the ground out of which discursive expression grows. She calls it the "natural instrument" of abstract thinking. She argues that all new ideas must first be expressed metaphorically, that is directly, before they can be named or defined. Thus she contends that metaphor or iconic meaning is logically prior to literal or non-iconic meaning.

"When we use a word for breath to
mean the element of life, we use it
metaphorically, just as when we use
words like "brillience", "enlighten-
ment", and other expressions literally
referring to light, to denote intelligence. Originally these are all metaphors directly conveying an image; and
it is the image that expresses the new
insight, the nameless idea that is
meant. The image, the thing actually
named, is the literal meaning of the
word; the metaphorical sense is the
new concept which (when it is first
encountered) no word in the existing
vocabulary literally denotes."[13]

In my judgement Ms. Langer is right-
headed in her efforts to offset the deep
and pervasive influence of logical empiricism in aesthetic theory. My concern is
that her way of going about this task is
not radical enough. For she tends to accept
the logical empiricist account of language
as essentially discursive and informational
in nature, while developing a parallel account of artistic expression. If we must
choose between (1) viewing art as strictly emotive and without cognitive meaning
and (2) a dualistic view which gives artistic expression a meaningful structure of
its own, parallel to that of discursive language, then the latter is the preferable
choice. But is there not a better way?

That Langer grants too much to the
logical empiricists at the outset is fairly easy to establish. Consider the fact
that she tends to define artistic expression,
together with the inner life of feeling which
it articulates, by contrasting them to linguistic expression with its subject matter of

15

outer, "scientific" and/or "practical" experience. By accepting this "established" account of the nature of language she unwittingly undertakes to do battle within the narrow confines of the opponent's home court. Along the same line, consider the vocabulary Langer uses to state her views. Human consciousness and experience are divided into "inner" and "outer" realms, and language is thought of as essentially "referential" ("the object named is the meaning of the word"); the primary function of language is said to be the "communication of information" and/or the symbolication of "public fact"; "statement" and "poetry" are contrasted and "metaphor is not language"; and finally, the logic or depth grammar of linguistic and artistic expression are said to be fundamentally distinct.

An examination of the three major contrasts which Langer draws between language and art will reveal more fully the extent to which she is dependent upon a positivist model of linguistic activity. As was mentioned earlier on, she speaks of language as representational or referential in character while designating art as presentational. This way of speaking harkens back to the logical atomism of Russell and the early Wittgenstein, hardly a solid base from which to launch an attack on the emotivist interpretation of aesthetics. Secondly, Langer maintains that art is expressive while language is discursive. Exactly what she means by the term 'discursive' is never made clear. In one passage[14] she equates it with the expression of 'rational cognition' and in another[15] she identifies it with the sequential presentation. But such moves create more confusion than clarity. For Langer most certainly considers

16

artistic insight a form of rational cognition and both music and drama (to say nothing of film and sport) are art forms based uniquely on sequential presentation.

Thirdly, Langer claims that art is iconic in character and language is not. By this she seems to mean that while language is properly speaking a symbolic activity, in that works symbolize or point to entities, works of art are not symbols in this sense. Rather, they embody or participate in the reality they symbolize; that is, they are not an image or replica of something else, their meaning is inherent within their being. Here again Langer's naivete concerning language becomes evident. Not only is the limiting of symbolism proper to cases of objective reference unnecessary and confusing, but the failure to acknowledge the deep inconic power of much linguistic activity (e.g. ritual, slogan, personal names, etc.) is most unfortunate. In addition, Wittgenstein's insights concerning the mediation of linguistic meaning through use in context renders Langer's sharp cleavage between language and the reality with which it meshes quite untenable.

There are two aspects of Langer's position which carry potential for a sounder view of language in general and of metaphor in particular. When discussing the confluence of art and language in poetry, she admits that the semantic study of poetry is valuable, but goes on to argue that a more promising approach would be to move from poetry to semantics - "Poetry exhibits, like nothing else in the world, the formulative use of language; it is the paradigm of creative speech. For the poetic use of language is essentially formulative use of language; it is the paradigm of creative speech. For the poetic use of language is essentially formulative."[16]  Earlier Langer analyzed the formulative function of language in the following fashion:

> "It is normally coincident with the communicative functions, but largely independent of them; and while its most spectacular exhibition is in poetry; it is profoundly, though not obviously, operative in our whole language-bound mental life."[17]

Likewise, it will be recalled that Langer views metaphor as the common matrix of both discursive and presentational thought.  If Langer were to follow this insight more thoroughly in her approach to the nature of language, it would lead to a far more comprehensive and fruitful view.  To maintain both that language is at bottom grounded in metaphor and that it is essentially representational and sequential is to argue at cross purposes with oneself.  It would be better to argue that metaphoric speech is logically prior to literal or strictly representational speech because the procedural rules necessary to the construction and learning of the latter can only be formulated in the former.  The rough-hewn open-textured character of ordinary language is the necessary ground of all precise and logical communication, for we have to stand somewhere in order to begin the process of making things "clear and distinct"--and that "somewhere" cannot itself be clear and distinct.  Thus discursive expression is parasitic on metaphoric expression.

Having once come to this insight, Langer should have seen that her neat dichotomy between the discursive and expressive utterance simply will not do.  What is needed is a view of both language and artistic  expression which makes the most of their common ground and insists that each be understood in terms of the other rather than as "separate but equal" modes of expression. Such a view would lessen the tendency of empiricists to obtain a corner on the "meaning market" and of artists to con us into accepting the notion of art as purely "personal statement". The fact-value split that now characterizes our culture is as insidious as it is pervasive, and Langer's dich-otomized view ultimately contributes to, rather than lessening, this split.

The second aspect of Langer's overall pos-ture which holds potential for the development of a sounder view of both language and artistic expression is her emphasis on the <u>presentational</u> mode of expression. Unfortunately she limits this mode to artistic endeavor, failing to acknowledge the possibility that language also has a powerful presentational dimension. The other side of this coin is, of course, the possibility that artistic expression can also participate in the communica-tive or informational process. Langer's limiting of each of these aspects of human expressive acti-vity to language and art respectively does violence to the holistic and integrated character of the human form of life. People do not shift gears like a science-fiction computer, now uttering discur-sive informatives, now presentational expressives. Our various activities, be they linguistic or ar-tistic, take place in concrete contexts which com-prise the warp and weft of our lives, and thus they participate in many expressive dimensions simultaneously. In a word, all of our behavior is polysignificant.

All of this brings us back to Langer's view that art uniquely provides a direct presentation of the felt, or emotional life. She has striven so hard to give artistic expression a life of its own, parallel to that of linguistic expression,

that she has dichotomized thoughts from feelings
and talks about the latter as if they took place
in a subjective vacuum.  People just do not have
an emotional and/or value-centered life which
flows along by itself.  We have feelings about
things and persons and events; we value this
above that in the context of our everyday lives.
In like manner, art certainly does mesh with our
emotional life, but only in and through the perceived world of things, persons, and events.  It
speaks from and to the whole person.  And converse-
ly, language too meshes with and evokes our emotions; it is not the limited form of communication
Langer thinks it is.

Further, Langer's claim that linguistic expression is indirect, because it is discursive,
while artistic expression is direct because it is
presentational simply will not hold up.  For artistic expression and awareness are mediated by means
of perception and convention, as E.H. Gombrich and
J.J. Gibson have clearly established.[18]  Moreover,
language is not indirect in the way Langer thinks
it is.  There is nothing hidden "behind" linguistic expression (in the mind of the speaker) which
constitutes its meaning, nor are the objects about
which people speak the meaning, once-removed, of
those utterances.  Meaning is a functional reality,
not a "substantive" one.  Linguistic meaning is
every bit as accessible or "direct" as artistic
meaning--and artistic expression is every bit as
mediated as linguistic expression.  Finally, when
it comes down to the specifics of metaphor, Langer
is at once confused and confusing.  Her "official"
position would seem to place metaphoric speech
outside of language, along with presentational expression.  And yet her intuition that somehow metaphor lies at the base of both the representational
and the presentational modes provides a spring-
board for a far more profound and comprehensive
approach.  Unfortunately Ms. Langer herself backs

away from this insight - or at least she has not
proceeded with its development.


### 3. Colin Turbayne

In his book The Myth of Metaphor,[19] Colin
Turbayne develops an approach to the notion of
metaphor which is quite distinct from the views
already discussed, but one which in the end takes
us no further. It can, in fact, be argued that
while his approach is more comprehensive in scope
than the others,it ultimately leads to the dead
end of skepticism. Moreover, it would seem that
Turbayne's position exemplifies the very weakness it seeks to pinpoint, that the exposer is the
exposee. In the final analysis, Turbayne's understanding of metaphoric expression hinges on an absolute dichotomy between literal, factual speech
and figurative, symbolic speech.

Under the rubric of metaphor Turbayne class-
ifies models, allegories, parable, fables, myths
and the like - all modes of thought and speech
which involve "the pretense that something is the
case when it is not", whether for explanation or
illustration. Turbayne's aim is neither to ban the
use of metaphor, nor to insist on the "translata-
bility" of every metaphoric utterance into factual
discourse. He contends not only that metaphor is
a useful explanatory device, but that we cannot
avoid using it. His concern, rather, is to stress
the importance of remembering that a metaphor is
(only) a metaphor, not a literal account of the
facts.

Whenever (frequently) metaphors are taken as
literally true, the thought of those who use them
is held captive by them and this is a "myth" that
needs exposing. Turbayne offers the dualism of the
"ghost in the machine", the representative theory

21

of perception, and the mechanical view of the
universe propounded by Descartes and Newton as
examples of metaphors being taken as literal
truth and in need of "demythologizing." His
technical term for metaphorical thought is
"sort-crossing" and mistaking metaphor for factual description is labeled "sort-trespassing".
There are obvious similarities between his moves
here and those of Gilbert Ryle with respect to
"category mistakes", though there are important
differences as well.

Turbayne does not recommend the positivist
method of exposing metaphors for what they are
by reducing them to literal speech. In fact, he
explicitly states that we can never know or state
what the facts of any situation actually are:
"We cannot say what reality is, only what it seems
like to us...we never know exactly what the facts
are." Rather, Turbayne advocates the sophisticated maneuver of revealing a metaphor as a (mere)
metaphor by offering an alternative metaphor which
does a better job of explaining the phenomenon in
question than the former one. The specific example he deals with is visual perception. He pro-
poses treating the events of nature as if they
composed a language and our coming to see them as
parallel to learning a language. He argues that
this way of explaining visual perception is as
good if not better than those explanations based
in geometric or mechanical models.

At a deeper and more general level, however,
the importance of Turbayne's approach lies in
the contention that metaphors are only metaphors,
not factual descriptions, and that even though we
cannot get beyond metaphors to the facts, we can
avoid being taken in by them through the continual
juxtaposing of alternative metaphors. Although we
cannot actually "demythologize" all metaphors, a
la Edwards, we can and must be vigilant in "remyth-
ologizing" them in order to keep ourselves from
being enslaved by them. It is precisely at this

deeper level, however, that certain conceptual difficulties begin to emerge, difficulties which render Turbayne's analysis fundamentally misleading.

The nub of the matter is simply that Turbayne has entangled himself in a trap of his own making. For on the one hand he wants to maintain that we are bound to metaphor, that we can only know reality through metaphorical thought and language, and that we can never know what the facts actually are. Thus we cannot demythologize, only remythologize the metaphoric mode. On the other hand, however, Turbayne contends that:

> And we need to guard against assuming that language mirrors the structure of the world. To help us in this last and other similar cases, I welcome Lord Russell's cure: "Against such errors," he says, "the only safeguard is to be able, once in a way, to discard words for a moment and contemplate facts more directly through images. Most serious advances in philosophic thought result from some such comparatively direct contemplation of facts".[26]

The difficulty here is that we are being told both that we are captive of metaphoric language and thought and that we need to transcend them. In fact, the insights which Turbayne offers, about the limitations of the metaphoric mode, are themselves presumably offered from a vantage point beyond metaphor. Moreover, we are not told how it is that we can "contemplate facts more directly through images" from a linguistic framework. It would seem that either we are bound by metaphor or we are not – but Turbayne seems to want it both ways.

23

Notes

--Chapter One--

1. <u>Systematic Theology</u>, I (Chicago: Chicago University Press, 1951),p. 238.

2. <u>Ibid</u>., p. 239.

3. <u>Ibid</u>., p. 239.

4. <u>Ibid</u>., p. 241.

5. <u>Dynamics of Faith</u> (New York: Harper and Row, 1958), p. 45.

6. Sidney Hook (ed.), <u>Religious Experience and Truth</u> (New York: New York University Press, 1961), p. 315.

7. <u>Mind</u>, April, 1965, p. 199.

8. <u>Problems of Art</u>, (New York: Scribners, 1957), pp. 132-133.

9. <u>Ibid</u>., pp. 7-8.

10. <u>Ibid</u>., pp. 133-134.

11. <u>Ibid</u>., p.148.

12. <u>Ibid</u>., p. 23.

13. <u>Ibid</u>., p. 105.

14. <u>Ibid</u>., pp. 124-125.

15. <u>Philosophy in a New Key</u> (Cambridge: Harvard University Press, 1957), p. 93.

16. <u>Problems of Art</u>, p. 151.

17. <u>Problems of Art</u>, P. 149.

18. E.H. Gombrich, <u>Art and Illusion</u>,(London: Phaidon, 1962) and R. Arnheim, <u>Visual Thinking</u> (London: Faber: 1969).

19. New Haven:  Yale University Press, 1962)

20. <u>Ibid.</u>, p. 100.

Chapter Two

--<u>Metaphor</u> <u>as</u> <u>Interaction</u>--


In this chapter the focus will be on views
of metaphor which emphasize the inter-relatedness
of various modes of speech rather than their
distinctness. In general the positions to be
presented have a three-fold advantage over those
discussed in the previous chapter: (1) they are
more in harmony with the way metaphor actually
functions in everyday conversation, (2) they are
subtle enough to do justice to the use of metaphor in aesthetic contexts, and (3) they are sufficiently sophisticated to encompass the scientific use of metaphor in model-building. For the
specific purposes of this study, these "interactionist" views of metaphoric discourse cast more
light on Wittgenstein's stance toward metaphor
than do those discussed previously.

Beginning with the views of Max Black and
Philip Wheelwright as compared and contrasted, I
shall then move to a consideration of the interpretations of Monroe Beardsley and Walker Percy.
The first two thinkers are primarily philosophers
by orientation, while Beardsley is more specifically an aesthetician and Percy is an eminent
novelist who occasionally writes on language
theory. Each is interesting in his own right,
and each contributes to an understanding of metaphor rich enough to provide a context for wrestling with Wittgenstein's mode of expression.


1.  Max Black and Phillip Wheelwright

At the outset of his account of metaphor,[1]
Max Black offers several examples of metaphoric
expressions and makes some general observations

about them.  He suggests that most often one word
or phrase in a metaphorical utterance strikes us
as being used in an unusual or unfamiliar way.
He thinks it helpful to call this word or phrase
the "focus" of the metaphor and to refer to the
remainder of the utterance as the "frame".  The
same focus term may appear within different
frames, thereby producing different metaphors.
In addition, Black asserts that it is necessary
to examine both the linguistic context and the
social setting within which a metaphor appears
in order to determine its meaning.  As with all
linguistic activity, metaphorical meaning very
much depends on such variables as emphasis (as
revealed through intonation, gesture, etc.) and
intention (as revealed through accompanying deeds
and results).

Next Black turns to an examination of the
"substitution" view of metaphor, according to
which a metaphorical expression is used in place
of its literal equivalent--either for convenience
or for ornamentation.  Black criticizes this view
on the basis that it fails to account for the
richness and complexity of many metaphorical expressions.  For the attempt to "translate" or
reduce metaphors to their literal equivalent
often is unsuccessful.  Sometimes, frequently
the more interesting and important times, a
metaphorical expression is used not as a conve-
nient or ornamental substitute, but as the most
direct and pointed way to articulate an insight.

Nor can the substitution view be salvaged by
falling back on a "comparison" view, wherein metaphor is explained as a truncated simile in which
an implied comparison is substituted for an explicit one.  For it is precisely this similarity
which an incisive metaphor captures, frequently
for the first time, and thus it will not do to
explain the metaphor in terms of the similarity.

Frequently similes follow after metaphors and thus the latter can hardly be explained in terms of or reduced to the former.

> Metaphorical statement is not a substitute for a formal comparison or any other kind of literal statement, but has its own distinctive capacities and achievements...It would be more illuminating in some of these cases to say that metaphor creates the similarity than to say that it formulates some similarity antecendently existing.[2]

Black draws upon the work of I.A. Richards in developing an "interaction" view of metaphor. According to this theory metaphor involves the use of a word or phrase in a context different from those within which it usually appears. By placing a fresh focus in an unfamiliar frame a speaker sets up an interaction between the associations that normally accompany each. Thus both our understanding of human nature and our conception of wolves are altered by the metaphorical expression "Man is a wolf". Of course, the primary thrust of the metaphor is directed at generating an insight about the former, with the wolf-associations reorganizing our conceptual as well as our emotional understanding of what it means to be human.

> Any human traits that can without undue strain be talked about in "wolf-language" will be rendered prominent, and any that cannot will be pushed into the background. The wolf-metaphor suppresses some details, emphasizes others--in short, organizes our view of man.[3]

Black concludes that although not all metaphors need to be classified as involving such interaction, the most powerful and effective ones are best thought of in this way because they will not submit to simple substitution or translation. Such attempts destroy the delicate balance which mediates the cognitive insight achieved by conceptual affective interaction. He maintains that when we attempt to reduce such metaphors to their "literal" meaning, the loss is not merely emotive but is as well "a loss of cognitive content. The translation fails to give the insight that the metaphor did."[4]

In a slightly different context[5] Black draws a likeness between the use of metaphor in everyday speech and the use of models in scientific endeavor. Here, too, he argues against those who maintain that models are simply picturesque and inexact ways of expressing insights which can, if the insight is true, be reduced or translated to more "rigorous" language. Black offers several key instances in which it is clear that highly productive insights have not been so reduced, even after much effort, and that practicing scientists take their models far more seriously than such a view would allow. Against those who concede that models and metaphors may be fruitful as heuristic devices but continue to insist that they must not be confused with the epistemological justification of scientific theories, Black maintains that effective metaphors also have an internal structure which "resonates" with the structure of the reality being dealt with. This is what makes them fruitful.

We have seen that the successful model must be isomorphic with its domain of application. So there is a rational basis for using the model. In stretching the language by which the model is

described in such a way as to fit the
new domain, we pin our hopes upon the
existence of a common structure in both
fields.  If the hope is fulfilled, there
will have been an objective ground for the
analogical transfer.  For we call a mode
of investigation rational when it has a
rationale, that is to say, when we can
find reasons which justify what we do and
that allow for articulate appraisal and
criticism.  The putative isomorphism between
model and field of application provides such
a rationale and yields such standards of
critical judgment.  We can determine the
validity of a given model by checking the
extent of its isomorphism with its intended application.  In appraising models as
good or bad, we need not rely on the
sheerly pragmatic test of fruitfulness in
discovery; we can, in principle at least,
determine the "goodness" of their "fit."[6]

Another helpful and somewhat similar, analysis
of metaphor is offered by Phillip Wheelwright.  He
begins by defining metaphor as a metamorphosis of
meaning at a deep level, brought about by the interaction of what he terms "epiphor" and "diaphor".
The former signifies the extension of meaning
through comparison of similarities while the latter designates the creation of new meaning by
juxtaposition and synthesis of dissimilarities.
Both diaphor and epiphor are most effective when
not treating obvious similarities or dissimilarities.

The best epiphors have freshness; they call
light attention to similarities not readily
noticed: they involve, in Aristotle's
phrase, "an intuitive perception of the
similarity of dissimilars."... the comparison

comes as a shock which is yet a shock of recognition...The essential possibility of diaphor lies in the broad ontological fact that new qualities and new meanings can emerge, simply come into being, out of some hitherto ungrouped combination of elements.[8]

The internal relationship between epiphor and diaphor is complex. Sometimes they can be alternated so as to repeatedly attack a subject from different perspectives, while at other times one may be used within the context of the other. Wheelwright gives the following examples of metaphoric expression and comments upon them:

(1)      My salad days,
    When I was green in judgment

(2) A bracelet of bright hair about the bone

(3) We have lingered in the chambers of
        the sea
    By Sea-girls wreathed with seaweed
        red and brown

That there is epiphor in each of the instances is shown by the felt subterranean power to mean something more than the words actually say. That there is diaphor is evident from the utterly untranslatable character of each utterance--the role of epiphor is to hint significance, the role of diaphor is to create presence.[9]

Elsewhere[10] Wheelwright approaches the notion of metaphor from a slightly different angle. He suggests that metaphor may well be the paradigm of figurative or expressive language, which he distinguishes from "steno-language". The latter is an abstraction in which the logical and representational features of

30

linguistic utterances are focused and idealized; rarely if ever is language devoid of the expressive dimension. Wheelwright characterizes this expressive dimension as employing such features as continuity between symbol and referent (as in onomatopeia), contextual variation, plural-signification (useful ambiguity), concrete universalization, indirection, "soft" focus, assertorial lightness (mult-valued logic), and paradox.

The crux of metaphoric expressiveness lies, according to Wheelwright, in the semantic tension created by its epiphoric and diaphoric qualities.

The essence of metaphor consists in a semantic tension which subsists among the heterogeneous elements brought together in some striking image or expression. Poetic language implicitly crosswaves multiplicity-in-unity and unity-in-multiplicity; it is tensive because of the precarious balance between two or more lines of association which it invites the imagination to contemplate.[11]

Wheelwright seeks to distinguish metaphor from simile, not on the basis of grammar, but at the semantic or meaning level. In simile two verbal expressions, each conveying an individual image, are joined. In metaphor, however, a single expression conjoins two or more images to produce a unitary meaning. Thus in the former the vehicle is plural and the meaning is singular, while in the latter the vehicle is singular and the meaning is plural. Here again, however, Wheelwright stresses that the most effective expressive language results from the use of both simile and metaphor together.

There are a number of important similarities between the views of Black and Wheelwright. One of the more important of these is the notion of

interaction and/or tension lying at the heart
of metaphor. Another is their shared conviction
that metaphor is capable of carrying deep cognitive significance which cannot be communicated
in more "straightforward" language. Perhaps the
most important differences between the views of
Black and Wheelwright stem from their distinct
angles of approach. Black is concerned with the
place and meaning of metaphor in ordinary and
scientific language, while Wheelwright focuses
on the contrast between these two uses of language and the poetic-religious use. Their differences are not so much substantive as per-
spectival.

In spite of the superiority of the interactionist approaches of Black and Wheelwright
over those taken up in Chapter One, however,
there remains at least one major problem area,
more implicit than explicit, in their treatment
of metaphor. While they go a long way toward
undermining the pervasive positivist dichotomy
between cognitive and emotive language (by stressing the polysignificatory and interactive character of language in general), they do not offer
a concrete account of how metaphoric expressions
do in fact carry cognitive meaning. What is
needed is an epistemological schema for treating the inner logic of metaphor in a manner which
displays its distinctive cognitive character.
This is an issue to which we shall return from
time to time, and with which I shall deal directly to in Chapter Eight.


## 2.   Monroe Beardsley

The hallmark of the views discussed in the
first chapter is an unbridgable dichotomy between the cognitive and non-cognitive functions
of language. In such a context metaphorical expression generally receives short shrift. The
views of Wheelwright and Black, as presented in

the previous section, go a long way toward
overcoming the limitations of such a dichotomy, and the theory of metaphor developed
by Monroe Beardsley is more helpful still.
A brief exposition of his position, as set
forth in his classic, Aesthetics,[12] will
demonstrate both the reality and the specific nature of this helpfulness.

Beardsley slices the linguistic pie
quite differently. Beginning with the sentence, rather than the word, as the vehicle
of meaning, he distinguishes between what a
statement "states" and what it "suggests".
For example, the statements (1) "A republic
has been declared and the king has committed
suicide" and (2) The king has committed suicide and a republic has been declared" say
the same thing but suggest quite different
causal connections. It is precisely this
suggestibility within ordinary discourse on
which, according to Beardsley, the metaphoric
mode capitalizes. He also stresses that understanding a literary work as a whole is simply
an example "writ large"[13] of the metaphoric
dynamic on the sentence level.

In Beardsley's view the metaphoric mode
invites the hearer to explore the possibilities of meaning inherent within the creative
utterance without specifying in advance what
these possibilities are. Two principles regulate this exploration, "fittingness" (selec-
tion) and plentitude. There are, to be sure,
limits to the potential meanings of a given
metaphoric utterance, but within those limits
there exists, in the more powerful metaphors,
a vast richness of meaning.[14] The hearer must
play, according to the principles of fittingness, the meaning of the terms of the two main

33

categories chosen, off against the principle
of <u>plenitude</u>, by which meaning is multiplied
in terms of the open-textured nature of speech.
Metaphor exists on the threshold between established meaning and non-sense, continually turning the latter into the former. The hearer is
invited to explore the various signification
possibilities inherent within a given metaphorical utterance, even and perhaps especially
those involving logical absurdity. By means of
these dynamics metaphor can be said to "produce"
meaning, and the possibilities for such produc-
tion seem limitless and indispensable within
the body of living speech.

In a recent article[15] Beardsley discusses
one important aspect of metaphysical signification which often goes unmentioned. Generally,
if not almost exclusively, metaphors are examined in terms of the established meanings of
the terms involved and the intentions of the
speaker. Beardsley notes that attention must
be paid as well to the empirical knowledge of
the hearer, and to the possible discrepancies
which may arise between such knowledge and that
of the speaker. He deals with these factors in
terms of what he calls "credence-properties",
suggesting that the variability ratio between
what the speaker believes is characteristic of
a given object or category and what a hearer
believes makes it helpful to speak (as diction-
aries frequently do) of the various "metaphorical senses" of a term or expression.

Here again the strength of Beardsley's
analysis resides in his acknowledgement of what
might be termed the "flexibility zone" which
surrounds each use of metaphorical speech. The
transfer or conversion of meaning by means of
metaphor, while sufficiently predictable to

34

ensure communication, can only take place within a kind of indeterminacy on the part of both the speaker and the hearer. The significance of a metaphoric utterance, and indeed of metaphor in general, pivots on a reciprocal interaction between the terms and categories comprising the utterance per se, and between the beliefs, knowledge, and intentions of the speaker on the one hand and the beliefs, knowledge, and imagination of the hearer on the other hand.

There can be no question that throughout his analysis and exploration of the nature of metaphor Beardsley maintains that metaphorical speech can be cognitive in character. He argues, along with Black, that "translation" and "substitution" tactics do not do justice to the depth of meaning often carried by a metaphor. In fact, the specifically paradoxical structure of metaphoric expression defies such reductionistic moves, since one must grasp the meaning of the metaphor prior to and independently of substitutions and translations in order to make them. In the recent article referred to above, Beardsley defends the propriety of judging metaphorical utterances as "true" or "false".

> If the referent(s) of the subject of a metaphorical statement does in fact have all the properties of the intension of the metaphorical predicate, I see no bar to calling the statement "true". In many cases, of course, the referent(s) will have only some of those properties, so the statement will be false. Yet if many of the properties are there--those most important to that context--we may say the statement is "largely true" (the way we would with a complex historical narrative

that includes some errors but is right
about the main things)--or, if one likes,
"apt." It is an apt description of the
Nixon administration to say that it was
the high-water mark of the imperial presi-
dency, though like most metaphors isolated
from a context this also contains some
untruth.[16]

In spite of the power and insight of Beardsley's exposition there remains a sense in which
his account, like most of those already examined,
fails to cut deep enough to do justice to the
richness and centrality of metaphorical expression. Greater attention needs to be paid to the
relation between language in general, and metaphorical language in particular, on the one hand
and "the world" or reality on the other. This
will be the theme of those views taken up in
Chapter Three. The views of Walker Percy will
be discussed in the next section of the present
chapter, as a sort of transition between the
foregoing explorations and those yet to come.
Percy is essentially in "interactionist",
albeit with a perspective uniquely his own.


### 3. Walker Percy

Walker Percy is a contemporary Southern
novelist whose work is held in high repute by
writers and critics alike.[17] It is perhaps
as important as it is refreshing to encounter
a view of language proposed by a first-rate
literary artist -- a person whose life is given
to the careful use of metaphor--rather than
those propounded by philosophers and the like.
Moreover, Percy is far from naive with respect
to philosophical and linguistic research and
insight. Many of his essays, collected in a
book with the title, The Message in the Bottle,[18]

have appeared in important and learned journals in these fields. Indeed, his range of knowledge and depth of understanding make it a pity that his theoretic work is not more widely known.

The <u>locus</u> <u>textus</u> for much of Percy's thought is the powerful and puzzling experience of Helen Keller -- which dramatically intensifies the experience of every participant in language-- when she grasped how language works, "the meaning of meaning". Percy ponders this paradigmatic experience, this reinactment of the birth of symbolic meaning, with great care and unabashed wonderment. His focal question is, "What happens when people communicate through language?" He examines the two dominant explanations on the contemporary market, the legacies of empiricism and rationalism, and finds them both unhelpful. Skinnerian <u>behaviorism</u> is too thin while Chomskian <u>transformationalism</u> fails to meet the central issue.

Percy's critique of Skinner's account of verbal behavior focuses on (1) inability to explain the child's capacity to understand, and indeed to hear, locutions previously unencountered (a point well developed by Chomsky) and (2) its failure to take into consideration the linguistic and social contexts of seemingly simple speech-acts. In short, the behaviorist model is not rich enough to bear the weight of actual linguistic practice. The critique of Chomsky's approach is also two-fold: (1) it ultimately falls back on circular reasoning (language acquisition is explained in terms of a child's ability to acquire language) and (2) it tends to ignore social interaction and contextual dynamics in favor of innate and invariable capacities. Percy contends that these two alternatives do not exhaust the possibilities with respect to coming to an understanding of language and meaning, the speech event.

Beginning with the insight that a simple, reductionistic explanation of linguistic activity, whether in terms of linear inputs and outputs or innate "deep structures", is inadequate, Percy takes as his starting point the irreducible _relational_ character of speech. The relationship is triadic in nature (what he calls "the Delta factor") among the hearer, the word, and the world. The intersection of these three dimensions of human experience constitutes language, and any attempt to explain it in fewer terms is bound to be a distortion. Linguistic communication, according to Percy, is fundamentally _interactive_, and must be understood as a complex whole or _Gestalt_. Drawing upon C.S. Peirce's distinction between dyadic and triadic events, Percy contends that the latter cannot be reduced to a series of the former, as the atomistic predilection of behaviorism and empiricism would urge.

In his essay entitled, "A Triadic Theory of Meaning", Percy stresses a number of social interactionist and Wittgensteinian themes: (1) ultimately it is _speakers_, not words, which _mean_, (2) meaning is _mediated_ through _use in context_, (3) all language takes place _in community_, (4) all communication takes place in a _world_, (5) all speech has a _normative_ thrust, (6) every speech-act is capable of being _misunderstood_, and (7) it is frequently the _mode_ of a given speech-act which is mis-taken. Throughout his explorations Percy gives the impression of drawing heavily both from the continental phenomenology of the likes of Merleau-Ponty and from the British linguistic analysis of such as J.L. Austin. At all points the stress is on the _relational_ and _performative_ character of linguistic communication.

At a later point in his work, working
from the insights of George Herbert Mead and
Martin Buber as well as against those of Ogden
and Richards, Percy strengthens his basic insight by altering the triadic relation to include the speaker as well as the hearer, the
word, and the world.  So his more comprehensive
model is tetradic in nature.  Each and every
speech-event involves an irreducible interaction amongst speaker, hearer, speech, and
that  which is spoken about.

> Although the semiotic triangle is a
> useful model of stimulus-response arcs
> and of learning behavior, the fact is
> that symbolic behavior is irreducibly
> tetradic in structure...the second per-
> son is required as an element not merely
> in the genetic event of learning language
> but as the indispensable and enduring con-
> dition of all symbolic behavior.  The very
> act of symbolic formulation, whether it be
> language, logic, art, or even thinking, is
> of its very nature a formulation for a
> someone else.  Even Robinson Crusoe, wri-
> ting in his journal after twenty years on
> the island, is nevertheless performing a
> through-and-through social and inter-
> subjective act.[19]

The heart of Percy's understanding of linguistic communication lies in his distinction between a sequence and a pairing, between a linear
process and an act of coupling.  He sees both
the behaviorist and the transformationalist as
hung-up on an atomistic, sequential analysis of
what is essentially a wholistic, integrative
act.  The following quotation both clarifies his

meaning at this juncture and places him in relation to current linguistic theory:

> Once it becomes clear that what is to be
> studied is not sentence forms but particular
> language events, it also becomes clear that
> the subject of investigation in this instance
> is not the sentence itself but the mode in
> which it is asserted. The sentence can be
> studied only by a formal science such as
> grammar or logic, but a sentence event is
> open to a rich empirical phenomenology
> that is wholly unprovided by what passes
> currently as semantics. Nor can a neo-
> behavioristic psychology make sense of
> assertory behavior; it can only grasp a
> sequence of space-time events which it
> attempts to correlate by constant func-
> tions. But assertion--the giving of a name
> to a thing, this is water, or the declaring
> of a state of affairs, the water is cold--
> is not a sequence. It is a pairing or iden-
> tification of word and thing, class and
> thing, thing and attribute, and so on.
> Stimulus and response events are studied
> by a quantitative science. But the quasi
> identification events of symbolic behavior
> can be grasped only by a qualitative pheno-
> menology. This qualitative scale must take
> account not only of true-or-false-or-non-
> sense statements (water is cold, water is
> dry, water is upside down), but also of
> various modes of magic identification. It
> does not suffice, for example, to say that
> the assertions of a Bororo tribesman of
> Brazil, "I am a parakeet," is false or non-
> sense. Nor is it adequate to say that it
> is false scientifically but true mythically.
> It is necessary to understand the particular
> mode of identification or a particular lan-
> guage event.[20]

With this introduction to Percy's general
understanding of language we are in a position
to take a closer look at his view of metaphor
as a particular kind of word-event.  In an essay
intitled "Metaphor As Mistake" Percy approaches
the subject from a novel, albeit most provocative
angle.  He begins by examining several linguistic
errors which somehow have become accepted, either
in an individual's imagination or in local speech
conventions, and which serve as bearers of metaphorical meaning.  From this vantage point he
undercuts the common (among both philosophers and
linguists) assumption that when all is said and done
metaphoric speech is a form of mistake.  For even
when metaphoric utterances are based on mistakes
this observation hardly explains their function or
their power.

Percy makes it quite clear that in his view
a metaphoric utterance involves an interaction
between what is understood by the conventional
pairings in question and the creative juxtaposing of such traditional couplings.  The fresh
pairing calls attention to an aspect of experienced reality which had hitherto gone unnoticed.
The thrust and direction, and thus the significance, of the metaphoric interaction is provided
by the context surrounding the utterance.  As
Percy puts it:

> An unvarying element in the situation
> is a pointing at by context.  There must
> occur a preliminary meeting of minds and
> a mutually intended subject before any-
> thing can be said at at all.The context
> may vary all the way from a literal point-
> ing-by-finger and naming in the aboriginal
> naming act, to the pointing context of the
> poem which specifies the area where the
> metaphor is to be applied.  There is a
> reciprocal relationship between the select-
> ivity of the pointing and the univocity

of the metaphor: The clearer the context
and the more unmistakable the pointing,
the greater latitude allowed the analogy
of the metaphor. The aboriginal naming
act is, in this sense, the most obscure
and the most creative of metaphors; no
modern poem was ever as obscure as Miss
Sullivan's naming water water for
Helen Keller.[21]

According to Percy there are at least two
separate levels of metaphor, of what he terms
"analogy-making". There is the customary metaphor, "the saying about one thing that it is
something else...", and there is a more primordial level of naming wherein the sound of the
name bears an analogical resemblance (resonance?)
to that which is named. Percy thinks it is no
accident that certain crucial terms within all
Indoeuropean languages have the same roots (plu
for flowing and sta for standing, for example).
He suggests that this confluence of sound and
meaning is the bedrock of metaphor in particular
and linguistic meaning in general, and that it
is similar to perceptual synesthesia, the basis
of all empirical knowledge.

Throughout his discussion of metaphor Percy
makes it quite clear that he affirms the cognitive status of metaphoric communication. In
fact he contends that it is only by what he calls
"ontological pairing" that we can come to know
the world. For it is only through speech that we
share in each other's experience, and knowledge
is an intersubjective phenomenon.

> Without getting over one's head
> with the larger question of truth,
> one might still guess that it is
> extraordinarily rash of the posi-
> tivist to limit truth to the logical
> approximation--to say that we cannot
> know what things are but only how

they hang together. The copy theory
gives no account of the what we are saying
how about. As to the what: since we are
not angels, it is true that we cannot
know what it is intuitively and as it is
in itself. The modern semioticists is
scandalized by the metaphor _Flesh_ _is_ _grass_;
but he is also scandalized by the naming
sentence _This_ _is_ _flesh_. As Professor Veatch
has pointed out, he is confusing an instrument of knowing with what is known. The
word _flesh_ is not this solid flesh, and this
solid flesh is not grass. But unless we call
flesh grass, we shall not know how it is
with flesh. The semioticist leaves unex-
plained the act of knowing. He imagines
naively that I know what this is and then
give it a label, whereas the truth is, as
Cassierer has shown so impressively, that
I cannot know anything at all unless I symbolize it. We can only conceive being,
sidle up to it by laying something else
alongside. We approach the thing not directly but by laying something else alongside. We approach the thing not directly
but by apposing symbol and thing.[22]

When he does confront "the larger question
of truth" Percy takes his cue (though _not_ his
lines) from Aquinas. He introduces the notion
of _mediation_ as the axis around which knowledge
revolves. Knowing is seen as an "immaterial
union" between the knower and reality as mediated through sensory experience of material
entities. Moreover, it is intersubjective and
dialogical in character. Both this community
dimension of the knowing experience and the
knower's relation to the known are immaterial
yet nonetheless real bonds.

This same epistemological pattern forms
the basis of Percy's understanding of linguistic communication in general (as with Helen
Keller) and of metaphoric signification in

particular. At bottom all speech is metaphoric in that it affirms an identity between two material entities (word and thing) which are not metaphysically identical. However, it is only through such linguistic activity that we come to know the world.

> In its essence the making and the receiving of the naming act consist in a coupling, an apposing of two real entities, the uttered name and the object. It is this _pairing_ which is unique and unprecedented in the causal nexus of significatory meaning. But what is the nature of this pairing? The two terms, it is clear, are related in some sense of identification, yet not a real identity. To express it in modern semiotical language, the water is conceived through the vehicle of the symbol. In Scholastic language, the symbol has the peculiar property of containing within itself in _alio esse_, in another mode of existence, that which is symbolized. Helen knows the water _through_ and by means of the symbol.[23]

These then are the views of metaphor offered by some important thinkers who can be classified as "interactionists". They agree in maintaining that metaphor is in some sense irreducible, that it involves a fruitful overlapping of conventional categories, and that it often carries cognitive insight, i.e. knowledge. In the next chapter we shall encounter some thinkers who while not denying any of these tenents want to go further with respect to the importance of metaphor to language, knowledge and reality.

1. "Metaphor", in <u>Models</u> <u>and</u> <u>Metaphors</u> (Ithaca: Cornell University Press, 1942.

2. <u>Ibid.</u>, p. 37.

3. <u>Ibid.</u>, p. 41.

4. <u>Ibid.</u>, p. 46.

5. "Models and Archetypes", in <u>Models</u> <u>and</u> <u>Metaphors</u>.

6. <u>Ibid.</u>, p. 238.

7. P. Wheelwright, <u>Metaphor</u> <u>and</u> <u>Reality</u>: (Bloomington: Indiana Univ. Press, 1962.

8. <u>Ibid.</u>, pp. 74 and 85, respectively

9. <u>Ibid.</u>, p. 91.

10. P. Wheelwright, <u>The</u> <u>Burning</u> <u>Fountain</u>, revised edition (Bloomington: Indiana Univ. Press, 1968).

11. <u>Ibid.</u>, p. 102.

12. (New York: Harcourt, Brace and World, 1958).

13. <u>Ibid.</u>, p. 115.

14. <u>Aesthetics, Op. Cit.</u>, p. 128.

15. "Metaphorical Senses", <u>Nous</u>, March 1978.

16. <u>Ibid.</u>, p. 15.

17.   Cf. "The Last man in America Who Believes
in Love", <u>Saturday</u> <u>Review</u>,

18.   (New York:  Farrar, Strauss, and Gireux, 19).

19.   <u>Ibid</u>., p. 200.

20.   <u>Ibid</u>., p. 205.

21.   <u>Ibid</u>., p. 78.

22.   <u>Ibid</u>., p. 72.

23.   <u>Ibid</u>., p. 261.

# Chapter Three

## --Metaphor As Constitutive--

At the opposite extreme from those who contend that metaphoric expression is cognitively expendable cluster those thinkers who take a stand even more radical than that of the interactionalists. There are those who maintain that in some deep, important sense metaphoric expression is constitutive of reality. The central thrust of this position is that the world of human experience is woven, at least partly, out of the structure of the language in which we speak and think -- and that the metaphoric mode lies at the center of the cognitive process. In short, in this view metaphor is taken to be logically prior to so-called "literal" speech. This chapter will be devoted to an examination of this approach.

I shall begin with a consideration of the view of Nelson Goodman. Next we shall turn our attention to the position of the French philosopher Paul Ricoeur on the relation between thought and reality. The chapter will close with a brief survey of the views of several other thinkers who in one way or another affirm that metaphoric speech is essentially constitutive of reality. Maurice Merleau-Ponty, Hans-Georg Gadamer, and Owen Barfield comprise the main points along this phenomenological spectrum.

## 1. Nelson Goodman

In his important and highly provocative book, Languages of Art,[1] Goodman takes a definite position on the relation between language and the world. He contends that far from being optional and arbitrary, language is <u>constitutive</u> of reality. Words and statements refer, to be sure, to the world, but not as mere labels and/or "pictures". Rather, language and reality participate in a mutually symbiotic relationship. More specifically, Goodman maintains that we are continually "remaking reality" by means of the language, especially the metaphors, we use in dealing with it. At the deepest and broadest level our basic symbols determine the structure and character of our world.

Goodman's position is essentially the diametric opposite of that taken by Paul Edwards and other logical empiricists. They view language as a passive mirror of reality while he views it as an active creator of reality. Edwards and others like him have what has been called "the luggage-tag" theory of language, while Goodman has what might be termed an "Orphic" understanding of symbolism, since he sees language as bringing the world to life. At the same time Goodman seems to go beyond even the interactionists, discussed in the last chapter, in his stress on the primordial quality of symbols in relation to the world. For him symbols not only <u>reveal</u> and evoke insight into reality, but they <u>create</u> it as well.

It is clear that Goodman stands with the interactionists over-against the substitutionists in emphasizing the <u>cognitive</u> character of symbolic and/or metaphoric expression. He stands four-square against the cognitive/emotive dichotomy so prevalent in contemporary thought, arguing that "In aesthetic experience the emotions function cognitively." In both science and art truth is determined on the basis of the "appropriateness" established between a given symbol system and the facts of experience broadly conceived. Moreover, metaphor is said to work by, and to be evaluated in terms of, the <u>transference</u> of meaning from one set or system of symbols to another. Goodman defines metaphor (metaphorically!) as "an affair

48

between a predicate with a past and an object
that yields while protesting... a happy and
revitalizing, even if bigamous, second
marriage".[2]

There is a pragmatist and nominalist thrust
to Goodman's theory of language in general and
metaphor in particular.  While stressing the referential and  cognitive character of symbols,
Goodman nevertheless insists that they are our
instruments for creating and engaging the world,
and thus in no way can be said to reflect the nature of reality.  Reality is linguistically constituted and is thus not ontologically prior to
symbols and/or metaphors.  Such a posture re-
sembles both the neo-Kantian motif of someone
like Ernst Cassier[3] and the pragmatism of W.V.O.
Quine.[4]  The sort of nominalism involved is far
from being flat, narrow, and impoverished.  It
is, rather, as complex and comprehensive as it
is rich in cognitive potential.

The conventionalism and/or relativism seemingly inherent in Goodman's theory of the relation between language and reality is faced up to
directly in his most recent book, Ways of Worldmaking.[5]  Therein he develops three main lines
of support for his seemingly irreverent and im-
prudent affirmation of a kind of "linguistic
relativity".  He argues for and from (1) a metaphysical pluralism, (2) an epistemological "relativism under rigorous restrainsts", and (3) a
theory of symbolic expression as cognitive.  A
brief examination of each of these lines of support will provide an excellent basis for understanding the main force of Goodman's view of
metaphor.

To begin with, Goodman takes as his axis
the notion that all descriptions of, or assertions about reality only have meaning within a
conceptual and/or linguistic framework.  Thus

49

facts themselves only exist within a theoretic structure or symbolic system, they are always "theory-laden" and not "pure".

> If I ask about the world, you can offer to tell me how it is under one or more frames of reference; but if I insist that you tell me how it is apart from all frames, what can you say? We are confined to ways of describing whatever is described. Our universe, so to speak, consists of these ways rather than of a world or of worlds.[6]

Goodman's view is <u>not</u> that we have multiple and alternative views of a single, actual world, but that we have multiple <u>actual worlds</u> which are constituted by the different visions and corresponding symbol systems developed within our various disciplines and dimensions of experience. These different worlds cannot and need not be reduced to one another or to a common ontological denominator. The worlds of science, art, philosophy, religion, and everyday discourse, to name several examples, neither describe the same world nor are they reducible to one another. The symbol systems appropriate to each are essentially self-contained and non-translatable. Goodman contends that even the "stuffs" out of which our many worlds are made are themselves made along with the worlds, not from nothing but from other worlds already on hand. Worldmaking is always a "remaking".

With respect to the question of the "truth" of our various efforts at worldmaking, Goodman affirms both the <u>relativity</u> and the <u>rigor</u> of epistemological criteria. Generally speaking the standard tests of coherence with "un-yielding beliefs and observations", internal consistency, simplicity, and comprehensiveness function as basic criteria. There are, however, according to Goodman no hard and fast lines between precepts and facts, no universally incorrigible "givens" which serve as the final test of truth. Nevertheless, there is always a difference between "rightness" and "wrongness", between what is fitting and what is not, in every worldmaking activity, whether it be science, painting, or philosophy. "A broad mind is no substitute for hard work".

> What I have said so far plainly points to a radical relativism; but severe restraints are imposed. Willingness to accept countless alternative true or right world-versions does not mean that everything goes, that tall stories are as good as short ones, that truths are no longer distinguished from falsehoods, but only that truth must be otherwise conceived than as correspondence with a ready-made world. Though we make worlds by making versions, we no more make a world by putting symbols together at random than a carpenter makes a chair by putting pieces of wood together at random. The multiple worlds I countenance are just the actual worlds made by and answering to true or right versions.[7]

In the final analysis Goodman falls back on knowing as a judgment-making activity, as providing the bedrock for truth. Certain claims are accepted as true because they are judged by the person or persons involved to fit within a well-proven worldview. Worldviews, in turn, and even worlds themselves, are accepted or lived within because they are recognized as appropriate with respect to the task of worldmaking. Such acts of judgment are neither final nor entirely relative; rather they are the necessary fulcrum for all knowledge. The skills and commitments of the knowing subject(s) cannot be ignored as

51

"mere Psychology". Without the practice and authority of judgment makers, neither worlds nor knowledge thereof would exist.

> We have seen, on the contrary, that rightness of categorization, which enters into most other varieties of rightness, is rather a matter of fit with practice; that without the organization, the selection of relevant kinds, effected by evolving tradition, there is no rightness or wrongness of categorization, no validity of inductive inference, no fair or unfair sampling, and no uniformity or disparity among samples. Thus justifying such tests for rightness may consist primarily in showing not that they are reliable but that they are authoritative.[8]

Goodman brings the foregoing ideas on reality and truth to bear on the notion of metaphor in the following manner. In addition to his concern to stress the cognitive character of metaphoric speech, especially at the constituative level of worldmaking, Goodman contends that the worlds made by and through the arts are every bit as "actual" as are those made by physicists, historians, and behavioral scientists. Whereas metaphor may not be at the forefront in the latter (though its always at the fulcrum), it is clearly the main concern in the former. The worlds created by musicians, painters, and writers are "real" and thus the metaphoric moves whereby they are constituted serve as bearers of knowledge.

> Fiction, then, whether written or painted or acted, applies truly neither to nothing nor to diaphanous possible worlds but, albeit metaphorically, to

actual worlds. Somewhat as I have argued elsewhere that the merely possible--
so far as admissible at all--lies within
the actual worlds. Fiction operates in
actual worlds in much the same way as non-
fiction. Cervantes and Bosch and Goya,
no less than Boswell and Newton and Darwin,
take and unmake and remake and retake
familiar worlds, recasting them in re-
markable and sometimes recondite but
eventually recognizable--that is re-cogniz-
able--ways.[9]

Goodman carries his "radical relativism
under rigorous restraints" even to a point of
applying it to his own views, to his own "outline of the facts concerning the fabrication of
facts". The truth of philosophical accounts of
"how things are" in various worlds and in worldmaking, as well as the truth of metaphilosophical
versions of the nature of such philosophical
accounts, is dependent on a flexible and relative application of such non-absolute criteria
as coherence, consistency, and fittingness.
When pressed to offer a justification of these
criteria themselves, and of his own advocacy of
them, Goodman replies that at such a bedrock
level justification consists more of <u>invitation</u>
and <u>persuasion</u> than of traditional argumentation.

> In such a context, I am not so much
> stating a belief or advancing a thesis
> or a doctrine as proposing a categori-
> zation or scheme of organization, calling
> attention to a way of setting our nets to
> capture what may be significant likenesses
> and differences. Argument for the cate-
> gorization, the scheme, suggested could
> not be for its truth, since it has no
> truth-value, but for its efficacy in
> worldmaking and understanding. An argu-

53

ment would consist rather of calling
attention to important parallels between
pictorial representation and verbal deno-
tation, or pointing out obscurities and
confusions that are clarified by this
association, of showing how this organ-
ization works with other aspects of the
theory of symbols.  For a categorial system, what needs to be shown is not that
it is true but what it can do.  Put crass-
ly, what is called for in such cases is
less like arguing than selling.[10]

Here again, then, Goodman stands out as an
example of a thinker who maintains the constitutive character of metaphoric speech, even and
especially at the level of justification of
worldviews in general and of philosophical
visions in particular.  For Goodman the worlds
in which we live are made, and they are made
through the employment of concepts and metaphors
under the watchful eye of certain flexible
criteria.  Even these criteria are justified
and thus constituted by appeals to their use-
fulness in the process of worldmaking.


## 2.  Paul Ricoeur

Ricoeur's recent, encyclopedic, and highly
provocative study, The Rule of Metaphor undertakes to trace the history of the notion of
metaphor from Aristotle to contemporary times.
He begins by outlining and then critiquing the
"substitution" theory of metaphor.  The major
difficulty with this theory is its assumption
that the unit of meaning in language in general
and metaphorical speech in particular is the
word.  Moreover, this assumption is commonly
conjoined with the idea that words are essen-

tially names. Such a point of departure inevitably leads to the view that at best metaphoric speech is "translatable" into "literal" speech and at worst it is merely "word salad". This approach to metaphor falls by the wayside when it is realized that the fundamental unit of speech is not the word but the sentence, and that so-called "literal" statements are themselves merely dead metaphors.

Ricoeur then moves to a consideration of "interactionist" views of metaphor, such as those of Black, Beardsley, and Emile Benveniste. He parallels the distinction between the substitution and interactionist views to that between semiotics and semantics in linguistic theory. The first members of these respective parts focus on meaning as a function of isolated words within a syntactical system, while the latter stress the cruciality of relation and tension to the notion of meaning, especially with respect to metaphor. Ricoeur argues that the metaphoric mode creates meaning by engaging in what he terms "impertinent predication". The tension between traditional uses and utterances combined in a fresh manner gives rise to new insights into the world of experienced reality.

The heart of Ricoeur's analysis of this creative, impertinent predication lies in his treatment of the notion of resemblance and the function of the copula, is. Whenever we affirm a similarity between two or more aspects of our world, we by the same act simultaneously affirm various dissimilarities as well. Thus to say that chairs and tables are similar in that they are both kinds of furniture is at the same time to say that they are different in some respects as well; otherwise, there would be no need, indeed no basis, to bring them together at all, since they would be identical. In like manner,

to say, as did Winston Churchill, that "Russia
has dropped an iron curtain across Europe" is
to simultaneously affirm a positive and a negative relationship between Russia's political
policy immediately following World War II and
the separation between actors and audience
effected by a curtain. These two acts are both
similar and dissimilar. Thus the use of "is"
always cuts in two directions at once, especially
in metaphorical speech. For the fresh insight
only comes to light as a result of the tension
between this symbiotic tension.

In addition to agreeing with the interactionists as over against the substitutionists, however, Ricoeur also follows Nelson
Goodman in asserting the creative or orphic
force of the metaphoric mode. In his chapter
intitled "Metaphor and Reference" he draws upon
Goodman's "World-making" theory of metaphor and
argues against the sophisticated yet latent positivism of the likes of Suzanne Langer and North-
rop Frye. The former rejects, while the latter
accepts, a dichotomy between cognitive and emotive meaning which relegates metaphoric utterances to an epistemological and metaphysical
limbo. To experience a work of art as sad or
warm is not the same thing as experiencing a
person or room as such, but neither is it the
same thing as feeling sad or warm oneself.
There is some sort of real connection, albeit
a metaphorical one, being affirmed by the language clustering around such experiences. Indeed, the linguistic context even seems to provide the matrix or basic out of which these
experiences arise. In short, there seems to be
a sense in which it is proper to say that metaphoric speech constitutes our world.

The expression (sad), therefore, is
no less real than the colour (blue).

The fact that it is neither verbal nor literal, but representational and transferred, does not make the expression any less 'true', so long as it is appropriate. Expression is not constituted by the effects on the spectator, for I can perceive the sadness of a picture without being made sad by it. 'Metaphorical importation' is able to make this predicate an acquired property; the expression is truly the possession of the thing. A painting expresses properties that it exemplifies metaphorically in virtue of its status as pictorial symbol.[11]

At this point, however, Ricoeur sees himself as parting company with Goodman because the latter is content to draw only nominalist conclusions from the fore-going affirmations. For Goodman the world is exclusively a function of the metaphors and models we devise, and whereas we can make and remake our world through our language we can never claim that we have, or are getting closer to, a description of the "real world." The fittingness of certain ways of speaking, to Ricoeur's mind, can hardly be fully explained in terms of internal linguistic consistency.

Does not the fittingness, the appropriateness of certain verbal and non-verbal predicates, indicate that language not only has organized reality in a different way, but also made manifest a way of being of things, which is brought to language thanks to semantic innovation? It would seem that the enigma of metaphorical discourse is that it 'invents' in both senses of the word; what it creates, it discovers; and what it finds, it invents.[12]

Following Max Black, Mary Hesse, and
Stephen Toulmin, Ricoeur goes on to explore the
referential dimension of scientific models. In
addition, he returns to the conflicting positions of Wheelwright and Turbayne on the question of the "truth" of metaphoric speech.
Wheelwright grants too much to metaphor by implying that it has no cognitive limits, while Turbayne grants too little by insisting that metaphors are only metaphors. Ricoeur concludes
that the paradox necessitated by the inescapable,
two-fold assertion within metaphoric speech--
the "is" and the "is not"--suggests the acknowledgement of the referential quality of metaphor, and thus of its cognitive quality as well.

> I do not say that this twofold critique
> proves the thesis. The internal cri-
> tique only helps us recognize the
> assumptions and commitments of one who
> speaks and uses the verb to be metaphor-
> cially. At the same time, it underlines
> the inescapably paradoxical character
> surrounding a metaphorical concept of
> truth. The paradox consists in the fact
> that there is no other way to do justice
> to the notion of metaphorical truth than
> to include the critical incision of the
> (literal) 'is not' within the ontological
> vehemence of the (metaphorical) 'is'. In
> doing so, the thesis merely draws the most
> extreme consequence of the theory of
> tension.[13]

Perhaps another way to put the epistemological thrust of Ricoeur's conclusion is in
terms of Michael Polyani's notion of "universal
intent". Put generally, the point is that all
linguistic affirmations do, as a matter both of
logic and of fact, seek to state the truth,
("how things are") about their chosen aspect of

experienced reality (this statement itself is an excellent case in point). This is no less true of metaphoric speech than it is of non-metaphoric speech. In short, all affirmations intend to be taken as, directly aim at being, true universally. Even the statement "All truths are relative to a given culture (or individual)" is meant to be understood and agreed with as a universal truth claim. A case in point is B.F. Skinner's effort to describe "verbal behavior" exclusively as a function of operant conditioning, while at the same time proposing his description as a "true" account of the facts. At the foundational level of their work, all scientists either affirm that their fundamental models are true (or more true than their competitors), or they undercut the value of their own efforts.

To put this point specifically in relation to the discussion of metaphor, Ricoeur is maintaining that Goodman's relativism with respect to the question of reference and/or truth in metaphoric speech is self-defeating. For any account of how it is that we make and remake our world(s) by means of our models and metaphors aims at being a true account. This is true even if the account itself is based in metaphor at the bedrock level, as Goodman's at least occasionally seems to be. At the deepest level a true insight about the nature of things is being affirmed, intended, as universally acceptable--and other accounts are being affirmed as in some sense inadequate. The only way Goodman, like Turbayne, can express (expecting to be understood and agreed with) his point of view is by drawing on an implicit claim that it is possible to aim at the truth. Without this claim the affirmation implodes on itself.

The ontological thrust of Ricoeur's overall position might be construed in the follow-

ing way.  Although it may not be possible to
claim that reality can be described directly,
as with naive realism, it is not necessary to
jump to the opposite extreme and take on a
"linguistic idealism" which maintains that "the
limits of my language are the limits of my
world."  Even if one prefers to label his position as a form of pragmatism, as Goodman seems
to, it is neither necessary nor desirable to see
this posture as entailing linguistic relativism.
In making his case for the ontological significance of metaphoric speech, Ricoeur seems to
take up the position that speech and reality are
mutually constitutive of one another.  Since as
humans we are post-linguistic beings engaged in
embodied existence, it makes no sense for us to
speak either of reality in and of itself (Kant's
long-lost "noumena") or of linguistic meaning in
and of itself (à la Humpty Dumpty).  We use
speech in relation to reality and we know reality in relation to speech.

        A helpful model for understanding this view
of the intrinsic relationship between language
and reality might well be the symbiotic dynamic
of a magnetic force-field.  The poles which comprise this field are language and reality, and
yet neither can exist, let alone be understood,
apart from its relationship to the other.
Ricoeur would seem to be maintaining that at
this most fundamental level language is metaphoric, and that this metaphoric mode of speech
is constitutive of reality, not in the sense that
it totally determines it, but rather in the
sense that the respective poles of a magnetic
force-field can be said to constitute one another.  Moreover, since the metaphoric mode is
logically primitive in relation to our other
linguistic modes, it is by means of metaphor
that our deepest insights into reality can and
must be expressed.

## 3. A Phenomenological Spectrum

In a way the two thinkers previously discussed in this chapter, Nelson Goodman and Paul
Ricouer, represent the poles of an entire spectrum of thinkers who in one way or another affirm the constitutive character of metaphorical
speech. Between the relativism of Goodman and
the realism of Ricouer stand such writers as
Maurice Merleau-Ponty, Hans-Georg Gadamer, and
Owen Barfield. Although there is great diver-
sity amongst the views of these thinkers, there
is also a good deal of unanimity with respect to
the cruciality of language in forming and structuring reality. A brief review of their respective emphases will make this clear. But first a
word about Martin Heidegger.

In his later work _Heidegger_ became increasingly interested in language and its relation to
truth and reality. Moreover, he became convinced that at its base all speech is and must be
grounded in the _poetic mode_, that the only way
for reality to be known and spoken of is through
the "nonobjectifying" language of poetry. It is
not clear whether Heidegger was making a purely
epistemological point, about how reality must be
understood, or whether he was as well making an
ontological point, about how reality is constituted. He sometimes speaks as if the world and
speech are mutually interdependent, like the
relation between a forest and a clearing. At
other times he seems to think of poetic speech
more as the "uncovering" of an already and independently existing reality. It is this double
emphasis that makes a discussion and/or classification of Heidegger's position so very difficult, and that makes it advisable not to in-

clude him in the present survey.

The work of Merleau-Ponty gives a central place to the role of language in human experience. More pointedly, Merleau-Ponty maintains that the body and speech together form the matrix out of which our awareness of and inter-action with the world takes rise. Perception is primary, but perception must not be thought of as the result of independent, passive sensory processes. Rather, it is more accurately conceived of as an interrelated, synaesthetic inter-action between the body and the world taking place within a social and linguistic <u>mileau</u>. In short, for Merleau-Ponty human existence is comprised of <u>relationship</u>; relationship is logically prior or primordial to the self and the world as such. Physical and linguistic interaction constitute the warp and the weft out of which the self and the world are woven.

The axis for this relational interaction is the <u>embodied</u> character of human existence. In and through our bodies we become aware of and participate in, simultaneously, the vast and complex networks comprising the world. Speech is related to embodiment in that at the primordial level we first encounter and express meaning in connection with <u>gesture</u>, including the action of the tongue and throat, the face, the limbs, and posture. Because of the primitive and intimate nature of speech and embodiment, Merleau-Ponty affirms that language and thought are not to be understood as separate process in which the former represents the latter. Rather, thought is <u>directly expressed</u> in language. By means of speech we, in our bodies, engage the physical and social worlds, we take our place within them. Unexpressed thought and "private speech" are, to be sure, possible, but only as meta-moves, since they are logically parasitic on relational, "public" interaction.

With respect to the relation between speech and reality, Merleau-Ponty would seem to be more of a realist than a nominalist. He does not want to say that the world is strictly a function of the various models contained within and expressed by means of our conceptual activity. And yet he does maintain that reality is linguistically constituted in the sense that the world _for us_ is only known _as_ a world in and through our embodied and linguistic activity. Thus for Merleau-Ponty there would seem to be a _symbiotic_ relation between speech and reality such that each can only be _understood_ in relation to the other. Whether the world could be said to _exist_ independently of our relation to it is a moot question, since even the asking of it participates in and indeed presupposes our linguistic interaction with the world, both physical and social.

> Language certainly has an inner
> content, but this is not self-sub-
> sistent and self-conscious thought.
> What then does language express, if
> it does not express thoughts? It pre-
> sents or rather it _is_ the subject's
> taking up of a position in the world
> of his meanings. The term 'world'
> here is not a manner of speaking:
> it means that the 'mental' or cultural
> life borrows its structures from
> natural life and that the thinking
> subject must have its basis in the
> subject incarnate. The phonetic
> 'gesture' brings about, both for the
> speaking subject and for his hearers,
> a certain structural co-ordination of
> experience, a certain modulation of
> existence, exactly as a pattern of my

63

bodily behaviour endows the objects around me with a certain significance both for me and for others. The meaning of the gesture is not contained in it like some physical or physiological phenomenon. The meaning of the word is not contained in the word as a sound. But the human body is defined in terms of its property of appropriating, in an indefinite series of discountinuous acts, significant cores which transcend and transfigure its natural powers.[14]

Hans-Georg Gadamer has been primarily concerned with the process and problems of hermeneutic, or interpretation as it relates to understanding. In his efforts to explore and get a grasp on this process in relation to understanding both the world and other persons, Gadamer frequently uses the task of interpreting a text as a paradigm case. He draws heavily on ancient, and especially religious, texts in order to clarify the difficulties and principles involved in essential and comprehensive communication.

The over-riding theme of Gadamer's work is that of the crucial and primordial character of intersubjectivity, or "trans-subjectivity", with respect to all communication and understanding. Interpretation does not establish the connection between speaker and hearer; rather, such a point of contact is predicated on, can only be established because of, a previously acknowledged commonality of experience and shared life-form. To paraphrase Heidegger, at the fundamental level we do not speak in order to be understood, but rather because we are understood.

Gadamer's chief way of illustrating the basic and dynamic role of intersubjectivity in communication and understanding is by means of the phenomenon of game-playing. Like the later Wittgenstein, Gadamer employs the social give-and-take character of games to capture the participatory and dialogical qualities of linguistic expression and hermeneutic. There is a back-and-forth rhythm to all games, a rhythm which carries the participants along and which constitutes the real nature of the relationship between and among them. In order to understand any linguistic utterance, whether an ancient text or the comment of a friend, one must "play along" in this game (which is by no stretch of the imagination a trivial enterprise). Interaction is the key to understanding. Conversation, not abstract "propositioning", is the primary mode of speech.

By means of his own mode and manner of expression, as well as by his concern with conversation and religious texts, Gadamer clearly establishes his underlying commitment to the primordial character of metaphorical speech. Definitions, precise distinctions, and logical abstractions can only come, and need only come, about after more ambiguous, vague, yet adequate understanding has taken place. The initial insights embodied in metaphorical speech communicate this type of understanding. Gadamer is primarily concerned with hermeneutics at this level, rather than at the level reflected in the work of those discussed in the previous chapter who see metaphor as essentially interactive in character. He sees the relation between metaphorical language and reality as more of a symbiotic one, more closing paralleling Ricouer than Goodman. However, this symbiotic relationship is in a broad sense, a constitutive

65

one, <u>vis</u> <u>a</u> <u>vis</u> reality.

> Language is by no means simply an
> instrument, a tool. For it is in the
> nature of the tool that we master its
> use, which is to say we take it in hand
> and lay it aside when it has done its
> service. That is not the same as when
> we take the words of a language, lying
> ready in the mouth, and with their use
> let them sink back into the general store
> of words over which we dispose. Such
> an analogy is false because we never
> find ourselves as consciousness over
> against the world and, as it were, grasp
> after a tool of understanding in a word-
> less condition. Rather, in all our
> knowledge of ourselves and in all
> knowledge of the world, we are always
> already encompassed by the language that
> is our own. We grow up, and we become
> acquainted with men and in the last
> analysis with ourselves when we learn to
> speak. Learning to speak does not mean
> learning to use a preexistent tool for
> designating a world already somehow
> familiar to us; it means acquiring a
> familiarity and acquaintance with the
> world itself and how it confronts us.[15]

The main theme of much of <u>Owen Barfield's</u>
work is what might be called "the primacy of
metaphor". Barfield argues that contrary to
popular philosophical opinion, the metaphoric
mode is not ancillary to the discursive, but,
rather, the latter is parasitic on the former.
To borrow a notion from P.F. Strawson, Barfield
contends that metaphor is "logically primitive"
in the sense that it cannot be analysed into
constituent elements and it is the prerequisite
of all other forms of speech. Barfield's argument has three main aspects or lines of approach.

First, he notes an important etymological
anomaly.  On the one hand, general scholarly
opinion, as well as popular belief, has it that
language began with simple, representational
words which functioned as names of objects and
qualities, and that it has evolved through the
centuries by the steady accumulation of figurative, metaphoric expressions which are based
upon the more primitive, original meanings.  On
the other hand, it is generally acknowledged
by scholars in many fields that our present age
is but the latest stage in an increasingly less
poetic, metaphoric linguistic progression.  More
primitive ages, especially that of the early
Greeks, were clearly characterized by a high in-
cidence of mythological language and thought.
Barfield asks:

> ...if language had indeed advanced,
> by continual accretion of metaphor, from
> roots of speech with the simplest material
> reference, to the complex organism which
> we know today, it would surely be today
> that every author is a poet - today, when
> a man cannot utter a dozen words without
> wielding the creations of a hundred named
> and nameless poets...How is it then that,
> in actual fact, we find this almost uni-
> versal consciousness that the golden age
> of poetry is in the infancy of society?[16]

The second phase of Barfield's argument
begins by following Max Muller's suggestion
that there are two kinds of metaphor, the
"radical" and the "poetic".  The former are said
to be those wherein a single general characteristic is attributed to a wide variety of phenomena by employing the same word in referring
to them, as when we apply the term 'shine' to
sun, fire spring, thought, and joy.  Such
radical metaphors abound in early languages.

The poetic metaphors are, according to Muller, those wherein words which already having established and specific meanings are deliberately employed in relation to an heretofore unrelated situation. Even though he admires Muller's suggestion Barfield eventually rejects it because it is predicated on a distinction between general reference and specific reference. Such a distinction itself depends upon the assumption that originally each word designated a single thing whether it be a specific or a general thing. Barfield concludes that such analyses do not cut deeply enough because they do not go back far enough.

> To sum up, if we assume, as it seems
> only reasonable to assume, that in the
> ages of speech preceding anything that
> can be touched by modern etymology the
> main stream of language, whose course
> is afterwards to become plainly visible
> to us, was already flowing in the same
> direction (i.e. from homogeneity towards
> dissociation and multiplicity) and not
> in an opposite one, what is the result?
> Both 'root' hypothesis and 'metaphor'
> hypothesis fall to the ground together.
> Muller's so-called radical metaphor,
> instead of being primitive, is seen to
> be one of the latest achievements of
> conscious linguistic development. A
> better name for it would be synthetic
> metaphor; and a  better example, say,
> gramophone.  'Roots', far from being
> the germs of speech, are the product of
> ages of intellectual abstraction carried
> on, first, instinctively by ordinary
> speakers, and afterwards deliberately
> by the grammarians and philogists.
> The service rendered by these latter
> both to speech and to thought is of the

utmost importance; their error merely lay in supposing that life actually created language after the manner in which their logic reconstructed it. They mistook elements for seeds - and called them roots.[17]

The third and final aspect of Barfield's argument to establish the primary of metaphor is as simple as it is bold. He suggests that at the most fundamental level language is organ-ically related to reality, and that the meta-phoric mode of expression is our primary means both of interacting with reality and embodying this relation. At the primordial level words do not function as arbitrary and/or optional tags for various, ready-made, and isolated aspects of reality. Rather, they serve, along with our bodies, as our primary means of in-dwelling and participating in the world. Deep metaphors embody the dynamic structure of real-ity, while more analytic and specific modes of speech dismember it. Analytic speech clearly has its place, but the place of metaphoric speech is logically primitive to it. And thus, at this level, metaphors are constitutive of reality.

Men do not invent those mysterious relations between separate external objects, and between objects and feelings or ideas, which it is the function of poetry to reveal. These relations exist independently, not indeed of Thought, but of any indivi-dual thinker. And according to whether the footsteps are echoed in primitive language or, later on, in the made meta-phors of poets, we hear them after a different fashion and for different reason. The language of primitive men reports them as direct perceptual experience. The speaker has observed a unity, and is not therefore himself conscious of _relation_. But we, in the development of consciousness, have lost the power to see this one as one. Our sophistication, like Odin's, has cost us an eye; and now it is the language of poets, in so far as they create true metaphors, which must _restore_ this unity conceptually, after it has been lost from perception.[18]

This survey of widely differing theories about the nature of metaphor should provide sufficient background for carrying out the work that lies ahead. I have purposely ordered this survey to progress from less rich and less helpful views to those which are more sophisticated and comprehensive. This ordering will better enable us to place and discern the significance of Wittgenstein's implicit view of metaphor in Part Three. First, however, we must review Wittgenstein's _use_ of metaphor in his most significant writings.

## --Chapter Three--

### Notes

1. *Languages of Art*, (Indianapolis: Bobbs-Merrill, 1968)

2. *Ibid.*, p. 69.

3. Cassirier, Ernst. *The Philosophy of Symbolic Forms*(New Haven: Yale University Press, 1953)

4. Quine, W.O. *Word and Object* (New York: Wiley, 1960)

5. *Ways of Worldmaking* (Indianapolis: Hackett Publishing Co., 1978)

6. *Ibid.*, p. 3.

7. *Ibid.*, p. 94.

8. *Ibid.*, p. 138.

9. *Ibid.*, p. 104.

10. *Ibid.*, p. 129.

11. *The Rule of Metaphor* (Toronto: University of Toronto Press, 1977) p. 238.

12. *Ibid.*, p. 239.

13. *Ibid.*, p. 255.

14. *The Essential Writings of Merleau-Ponty* ed. Alden Fisher (New York: Harcourt, Brace and World, 1969) p. 206.

15. Hans-Georg, Gadamer, <u>Philosophical Hermeneutics</u>, (Berkeley: University of California Press, 1976) pp. 62-63

16. Owen Barfield, <u>Poetic Diction</u> (Middletown: Wesleyan University Press, 1973) p. 69.

17. <u>Ibid</u>., p. 81.

18. <u>Ibid</u>., p. 86.

PART TWO

Chapter Four

--Metaphors in the <u>Tractatus</u>--


In Part One I have traced our various postures with respect to the nature of metaphorical
speech.  The primary concern, in addition to
providing general background on metaphor <u>per</u> <u>se</u>,
was to raise and explore a number of different
issues that arise when the question of linguistic
meaning is approached.  Thus by means of a discussion of the metaphoric mode we have wrestled
a bit with the broader concerns of the philosophy of language.  Hopefully, too, a helpful
backdrop has been provided for better placing of
Wittgenstein's use of metaphor, which is the
primary concern of Part Two.

The best way to go about ascertaining how
Wittgenstein employed metaphor is simply by locating and clarifying the chief metaphoric expressions in his three most influential works,
<u>Tractatus</u> <u>Logico-Philosophieus</u>, <u>Philosophical</u>
<u>Investigation</u>, and <u>On</u> <u>Certainty</u>.  While there
will undoubtedly be some points of correlation
between the views discussed in Part One and the
present undertaking, the central focus will be
on introducing Wittgenstein's metaphors in and
of themselves.  The implications  of his use of
the metaphoric mode, in relation to the various
interpretive postures, will be the concern of
Part Three.

I. Logical Space and Place (<u>Logischen</u> <u>Raum</u> <u>Und</u> <u>Ort</u>)

The first major metaphorical expression in the <u>Tractatus</u> appears on the first page (1.13). It involves the notion of 'logical space'. This particular term appears six times in the first half of the <u>Tractatus</u> and not at all in the last half. Here are the instances:

1.13 The facts in logical space are the world.

2.11 A picture presents a situation in logical space, the existence and non-existence of states of affairs.

2.202 A picture represents a possible situation in logical space.

3.4 A proposition determines a place in logical space. The existence of this logical place is guaranteed by the mere existence of the constituents-- by the existence of the proposition with a sense.

3.42 A proposition can determine only one place in logical space: nevertheless the whole of logical space must already be given by it.
(Otherwise negation, logical sum, logical product, etc., would intro- duce more and more new elements--in co-ordination.)

(The logical scaffolding surround- ing a picture determines logical space. The force of a proposition reaches through the whole of logical space.)

74

4.463 A tautology leaves open to reality the whole--the infinite whole--or logical space: a contradiction fills the whole of logical space leaving no point of it for reality. Thus neither of them can determine reality in any way.

In the first instance (1.13) logical space is introduced as part of the explanation of the relationship between "the world" ("all that is the case") and "facts". The world is comprised, not of things, but of facts ("what is the case", "states of affairs"). Facts, in turn, are comprised of objects or things (2.01); they exist as a function of things but are not themselves things. For this reason they are said to occupy logical space rather than physical space (2.013). Since "reality" is broader than the world, including both what is the case (the actual) and what could be but is not the case (the possible), logical space is also occupied by "negative facts" (2.06).

The next two instances of this expression are essentially redundant of one another. In 2.11 a picture is said to present a situation in logical space, while in 2.202 a picture represents a possible situation in logical space. But the explanatory clause of 2.11, "the existence and non-existence of states of affairs", carries with it the notion of possibility and thus alleviates any tension that might initially suggest itself between these instances. The picturing metaphor deals with the relationship between reality and the human mind (and will be discussed in its own right shortly). Logical space, on the other hand, is offered as a characterization of the structure of reality itself.

Two further references to logical space occur in Wittgenstein's discussion of the nature of propositions (3.4 and 3.42). A proposition is said to demarcate a place in logical space and this place is then referred to as a "logical place". Logical place is a function of the relationship between its constituents, namely logical space and the particular proposition in question. Although a proposition can only designate one place in logical space, once this place is designated the whole of logical space is, by implication, thereby affected, at least negatively. A positive designation carries with it negative designations as well. To assert something is by the same act to assert that the opposite is not the case. This is the point of the other passage in which logical place is discussed (4.0641):

One could say that negation must be related to the logical place determined by the negated proposition. The negating proposition determines a logical place different from that of the negated proposition. The negating proposition determines a logical place with the help of the logical place of the negated proposition. For it describes it as lying outside the latter's logical place. The negated proposition can be negated again, and this in itself shows that what is negated is already a proposition, and not merely something that is preliminary to a proposition.

The relationships among a picture, a proposition, and logical space are addressed once again in 4.463. After having introduced the concept of truth-tables, Wittgenstein spends several pages discussing the nature of tautol-

ogies and contradictories. The former, because
they are by nature true in all cases, do not
designate any particular logical place within
logical space, while the latter function in
exactly the reverse fashion. A particular proposition (and here Wittgenstein suggests that
'proposition', 'picture', 'model' are all syno-
nymous), however, takes up a specific place in
logical space and thereby (negatively) restricts
other possibilities but (positively) provides
room for at least one actuality. Thus: "the
truth-conditions of a proposition determine the
range [in logical space] that it leaves open to
the facts."

This parallel between bodies and propositions, in physical and logical space respectively, is absolutely basic to the <u>Tractatus</u>. It is
worthwhile to note at this juncture that in
spite of its fundamental importance to almost
all of the other concerns of the <u>Tractatus</u>,
this parallel is never presented in a straight-
forward way, nor is it ever argued for. Rather
it constitutes the root metaphor upon which or
out of which these concerns grow and through
which they take their peculiar shape. I shall
return to this theme frequently throughout this
present work because it constitutes the focal
issue and particular burden of this study.
Suffice it to say at this juncture that I take
this lack of a systematic and analytic point of
departure to be a strength rather than a weakness. I do <u>not</u>, however, think that the author
of the <u>Tractatus</u> would have agreed.

A brief word about the genesis of this
spatial metaphor is in order. There seem to be
three related factors involved. The first is
geometry. Wittgenstein would seem to be working with a notion borrowed from Descartes'
analysis of geometric space in terms of inter-

secting coordinates:

> "In geometry and logic alike a place is
> a possibility: something can exist in
> it". (3.411) and "It is as impossible to
> represent in language anything that 'con-
> tradicts the laws of space, or to give
> the coordinates of a point that does not
> exist." (3.032).

The second factor is that of mechanics,
especially the work of Hertz:

> In a proposition there must be exactly
> as many distinguishable parts as in the
> situation that it represents. (4.04)
> The two must possess the same logical
> (mathematical) multiplicity. (Compare
> Hertz's <u>Mechanics</u> on dynamical models.)
> (4.04)

The third factor is Wittgenstein's remark
that his development of the picture theory of
meaning was triggered by a series of photos in
a magazine depicting the sequential events of an
automobile accident. All of these factors trace
back to Wittgenstin's early interest and training in engineering.

Two other brief metaphorical expressions
which relate to the notion of logical space
merit mention before moving on. When character-
izing states of affairs or facts Wittgenstein
says that they are comprised of objects (simples)
which "fit into one another like the links of a
chain" (2.03). Further on, he characterizes an
elementary (non-complex), proposition as a
"concatenation" of names (4.22). Thus there is
a one-to-one correspondence between propositions
as a chain of names and facts as a chain of
objects. Words name objects (and qualities) and

78

propositions picture facts. These objects and facts (both possible and actual) exist in logical space, the dimensions or range of which can be charted by means of truth-tables.

## 2.   Logical Pictures (Logische Bilder)

Between 2.1 and 3.01 we are given two and one half pages of propositions which assert the relationship between reality and thought to be one of logical picturing. Facts, both positive and negative, exist in physical space (the world) and logical space (reality). They are comprised of elements (things or objects) structured in a particular way. Thoughts are logical pictures or "models" (Modell) of these facts, they bracket certain aspects of reality as they exist in logical space and present them to the mind.

> The fact that the elements of a picture are related to one another in a determinate way represents that things are related to one another in the same way.
>    Let us call this connexion of its elements the structure of the picture, and let us call the possibility of this structure the pictorial form of the picture.  (2.15)

It must not be thought that Wittgenstein is offering a psychological account of what goes on in the mind when we think. He is using "picture", qualified as it is by 'logical', as a metaphor for speaking of the structural relationship between the world and thought, not as an account of the content of specific thoughts. Another way to state this is to point out that 'thought' is used in this context as a logical notion-- an abstraction roughly equivalent to assertion, statement, or proposition. This becomes in-

creasingly clear as Wittgenstein slides from discussing pictures to discussing propositions.
But more of this in a moment.

The relationship between logical pictures
and reality is characterized by yet another metaphor, that of the relation between a ruler and
the object measured. The picture "reaches
right out to" the object (2.1511), is "laid
against reality" (2.1512) so that "Only the end-
points of the graduating lines actually touch
the object..."(2.15121). This correlating relationship between the points on the ruler (elements of a picture) and the things comprising
a fact is dependent on there being something in
common between the two phenomena, namely "pictoral form" (2.17). "A picture has logico-
pictoral form in common with what it depicts"
(2.2). This stress on logical form makes it
clear that Wittgenstein is not discussing psychological images, i.e. mental content, but rather
the structure of thought in relation to reality.

When we stand outside of this relation and
analyse it, as in the case of the ruler alongside the object, we not only see the correspondence between the marks on the ruler and the
physical elements of the situation but we see
that the former correspond to the latter (2.1513).
That a picture represents the logical form of a
fact is not shown in the picture itself, but in
the act of picturing: "A picture cannot, however, depict (abbilden) its pictoral form: it
displays (weist sie auf) it" (2.172). Of course,
since any given picture of a fact (A) is itself
a fact (B) (2.141), we could presumably picture
to ourselves (B) the fact (C) that this picture
(B) pictures a fact (A), and so on.
Wittgenstein's general point is what might be
called an over-arching fact, namely that
thoughts do indeed picture facts; this is their

basic relationship to reality.

A slightly different way to put all this is suggested by 2.221: "What a picture represents is its sense". Here 'sense' (<u>Sinn</u>) or meaning is offered as a synonym for logico-pictoral form. Once again, the sense of a picture (or, to get ahead of ourselves a bit, a proposition) pertains to the elements of the factual situation and not to the fact that the picture represents their structure. The structure can be <u>said</u> (depicted) <u>in</u> the picture; <u>that</u> this can be and is said in the picture is <u>shown</u> (displayed) <u>by</u> the act of picturing. This identification of the sense of a picture or thought with its logical form is what gave rise to speaking of "the picture theory of meaning".

A picture is also said to be either true or false, depending on whether it agrees or disagrees with reality (2.21).

> The agreement or disagreement of its
> sense with reality constitutes its truth
> or falsity. (2.222)
> In order to tell whether a picture is
> true or false we must compare it with
> reality.  (2.223)

Although he gives no further analysis or account of this idea of comparision between thoughts and reality, it is clear on the one hand that (1) his understanding of truth presupposes some notion of experiential verifiability (3.1) and on the other hand that (2) he is not committed to the positivist verifiability criterion of meaning. In fact, since he readily distinguishes the sense of a picture from its truth or falsity (2.222) it would seem that he did not maintain that the latter is the ground of the former.

Beginning with 3.032 and 3.1 a subtle shift takes place in Wittgenstein's use of the logico-pictoral metaphor. Whereas he has been speaking of it in relation to thoughts, he now begins to speak of it in terms of 'language', and specifically 'propositions'. The connections between and among these concepts is not made explicit until 4. and 4.001: "A thought is a proposition with sense" and "The totality of propositions is language". Thus it seems that pictures find their natural expression in propositions, and just as facts fit together in logical space like links in a chain, so propositions which depict facts are more than a mere "medley of words" (3.141), they are like arrows in relation to points; points only indicate (name) while arrows give direction (have sense) (3.144).

Wittgenstein makes the equation of propositions and logical pictures complete when he says: "A proposition is a picture of reality. A proposition is a model of reality as we imagine it: (4.01). He likens the picturing function of propositions in relation to reality to that of musical and phonetic notation to music and speech, respectively."...these sign-languages prove to be pictures, even in the ordinary sense, of what they represent". (4.011). Further, after briefly developing the parallels between propositions and phonograph records, Wittgenstein says:

"The possibility of all imagery, of all our pictorial modes of expression, is contained in the logic of depiction." (4.015).

He concludes by stating that the essence of propositions is captured by hieroglyphic script,

"which depicts the facts that it describes"
(4.061).

Another important metaphor which Wittgenstein introduces when speaking of logical pictures couched in propositions is that of "logical scaffolding". Because a proposition "shows
its sense" (4.022) in the same way a picture does,
it can be spoken of as being surrounded by a logical scaffolding which establishes its place in
reality and thereby links it with all other
places--all possible and actual states of affairs (3.42 and 4.023). This logical scaffolding is expressed in the propositions of logic,
which while they do not represent or picture
facts, can be said to depict the relations between facts. "They have no 'subject-matter'"
(6.124). The logical relations depicted by the
propositions of logic--the structure of the
scaffolding of the world--can be worked out in
terms of "truth-tables" as Wittgenstein introduces them in 4.31 through 5.1311.

Frequently, when focusing on the difference between empirical propositions and logical
propositions, Wittgenstein makes use of a
mirroring metaphor. While states of affairs
can be pictured, logical relationships cannot;
rather, they are depicted in the act of picturing. Facts are represented in logical pictures, while the common logical form which facts
and pictures share shows itself in the juxtaposing of the two. It can be seen but not said
(in the picture or proposition in question)
that the one is the mirror-image of the other.
Of course one can formulate yet another picture
(a meta-picture) or proposition which pictures
the fact that the first proposition pictures
the original state of affairs, and so on. For
"A picture is a fact" (2.141). But the picturing
relationship itself must first be seen and not

<u>said</u> because a meta-picture can only come after
the original picturing.

> Propositions cannot represent logical
> form: it is mirrored in them.
> What finds its reflection in language,
> language cannot represent.
> What expresses <u>itself</u> in language, <u>we</u>
> cannot express by means of language.
> Propositions <u>show</u> the logical form of
> reality.
> They display it. (4.121)

Although they are very closely related,
there does seem to be an advantage in shifting
to the mirror metaphor from the picture metaphor when focusing on logical relations rather
than factual situations. In a sense a picture
can be thought of as having its own content
which, although it has the same logical form as
the fact it represents, may attract attention
to itself. A mirror, on the other hand, has no
content of its own other than the fact it represents and thus it displays the logical relationship between the two more purely (6.13).
A mirror calls attention to the duplicating
pattern more directly than does a picture (4.124).
The advantage of the mirror model is seen in
Wittgenstein's ensuing discussion of logical
negation (5.2-5.21)
For example:

> How can logic-all-embracing logic,
> which mirrors the world-use such peculiar
> crotchets and contrivances? Only because
> they are all connected with one another
> in an infinitely fine network, the great
> mirror.
> '-p' is true if 'p' is false. Therefore,
> in the proposition '-p', when it is true,
> 'p' is a false proposition. How then can

the stroke '-' make it agree with
reality?  (5.511-5.512)


3.  The Self as Limit (Das Ich Wie Grenze)

        Between 5.6 and 5.641 Wittgenstein employs
a series of expressions to speak about the relationship between the self, the world, and
language.  The basic point has to do with a
strict correlation between the limits of the
self's world of experience and the limits of the
self's language.  Since logic--the framework of
language--pervades the world and defines the
possible as well as the actual, the self cannot
experience anything outside the structure of
logic and language.  For to speak or think of
something presumably outside this structure involves using the structure, and thus what is
thought or said is not beyond the structure
after all.  Thus "The limits of my language
mean the limits of my world" (5.6).

        This point seems to carry with it the con-
clusion that "What the solipsist means is quite
correct; only it cannot be said, but makes itself manifest" (5.62).  And, "The world and life
are one" (5.621).  The difficulty that arises
from Wittgenstein apparently saying what he says
cannot be said will come up again shortly.  What
needs to be focused on now is that in refining
the above view, he seems to go even further and
argue not only that "I am my world" (5.63), but
that the self does not exist in the world as a
"subject that thinks or entertains ideas"
(5.631).  Rather, the self "is a limit of the
world" (5.632).

        Wittgenstein likens the relation of the
self to the world to that of the eye to the
visual field (5.633).  The eye is not a part of

85

the visual field, but rather lies outside it, at
(or, rather it _is_) the edge between the visual
field and nothingness or non-being.  In like
manner, the self, the knowing subject, is not a
part of the world, but rather functions as its
horizon.  This is not a psychological (scientific) statement but a philosophical (logical)
statement (5.641).  Actually, Wittgenstein says
that this view of the self sees it as a "metaphysical subject", in spite of the fact that he
has left no room in his overall view for speaking of metaphysical entities.  That his use of
this term can be understood in a Kantian sense--
metaphysics redefined as "critique", i.e. the
setting of the limits of thought and language--
does not allow him to avoid the problem, since
he has not, strictly speaking, left any room in
his overall view for talking about these limits.
They cannot be _said_, but _show_ themselves.  But
more of this in a bit.


4.  The World as "Network" (_die_ _Welt_ _Wie_ _Netz_)

        After initiating a discussion of the rela-
tionship between logic and the so-called "laws
of physics"--including "induction" and "causality"--Wittgenstein asserts the following:

        All such propositions, including the
        principle of sufficient reason, the
        laws of continuity in nature and of
        least effort in nature, etc. etc.--
        all these are a _priori_ insights about
        the forms in which the propositions of
        science can be cast. (6.34)

        Next, he employs an extended metaphor by
way of clarifying this assertion.  He suggests
that the business of describing the world is a
function of the relationship between what is to

be described and the structure of the system of description being used.

> Newtonian mechanics, for example, imposes a unified form on the description of the world. Let us imagine a white surface with irregular black spots on it. We then say that whatever kind of picture these make, I can always approximate as closely as I wish to the description of it by covering the surface with a sufficiently fine square mesh, and then saying of every square whether it is black or white. In this way I shall have imposed a unified form on the description of the surface. The form is optional, since I could have achieved the same result by using a net with a triangular or hexagonal mesh. Possibly the use of a triangular mesh would have made the description simpler: that is to say, it might be that we could describe the surface more accurately with a coarse triangular mesh than with a fine square mesh (or conversely), and so on. The different nets correspond to different systems for describing the world. (6.341)

One cannot help being reminded of Kant and his "categories of the understanding" when confronted with this metaphor of a "logical network". For in both cases what we come away knowing is a combination of the world as it is and the network through which we experience it. Wittgenstein concludes, in good Kantian fashion, that while the world known in this way tells us nothing about the world-in-and-of-itself ("das ding an sich"), the fact that it is possible to describe the world in precisely this way does tell us something about the world-in-and-of-itself, i.e., that it is describable in this way (6.342).

The manner and place in which this network metaphor is introduced seem to indicate that Wittgenstein meant to use it as an explanation of the ontological relation between logic and the "laws of physics". Although his initial use of the metaphor speaks specifically of Newtonian mechanics, it does imply that there might be other kinds of "nets" which might be used (Einsteinian, perhaps). Furthermore, he also speaks about such principles as induction, causality, and sufficient reason as being "about the net and not about what the net describes" (6.35). These principles would seem to run much deeper than a particular description of the world, such as Newton's. They seem to express the very framework of the logic and language we--at least in the West--must employ. Thus Wittgenstein would seem to be saying that even these "laws" are simply about how we come at the world, and are not about the world per se. And that there are no logical grounds for the justification of this way of coming at the world, since the very notion of logical justification is rooted in this way. (6.3631). Thus although we cannot help but think otherwise (and here Wittgenstein sounds more like Hume than Kant) "It is an hypothesis that the sun will rise tomorrow: and this means that we do not know whether it will rise" (6.36311).

Although there is no "factual necessity" that the sun must rise tomorrow, there does seem to be, in Wittgenstein's view, a "logical necessity: for us to use the network embodied in the principles articulated by induction, causality, non-contradiction, and the like (6.375). For this is what it means to think. Nevertheless, it remains an open question whether or not this network coincides with the way things are. This seems to be the point of the network metaphor. Once again it should be noted that within the account Wittgenstein has given of the relation between language and the world it is not possible to <u>say</u> the things he is saying <u>about</u> the relationship between logical necessity and factuality.

> If there were a law of causality, it
> might be put in the following way:
> There are laws of nature.
> But of course that cannot be said:
> it makes itself manifest. (6.36)

5. Value Lies "Outside: the World (<u>der</u> <u>Wert</u> <u>Ausserhalb</u> <u>der</u> <u>Welt</u> <u>liegen</u>)

In these last few pages of the <u>Tractatus</u> Wittgenstein turns his attention to locating value statements in relation to the schema he has devised for describing the relationship between language, thought, and the world. Since factual statements are all that are possible <u>within</u> the structure of logic, value statements must be placed "<u>outside</u>" that structure. What happens inside the realm of the meaningful is what is the case, anything else is not speakable (7). No propositions can be formed about something that is "higher" than facts (6.42).

> The sense of the world must lie outside
> the world. In the world everything is
> as it is, and everything happens as it
> does happen: <u>in</u> it no value exists--
> and if it did, it would have no value.
> If there is any value that does have
> value, it must lie outside the whole
> sphere of what happens and is the case.
> For all that happens and is the case is
> accidental.
> What makes it non-accidental cannot lie
> <u>within</u> the world, since if it did it

would itself be accidental.
It must lie outside the world. (6.41)

This eliminates, to begin with, ethical and aesthetic discourse from the category of the expressable. "It is clear that ethics cannot be put into words. Ethics is transcendental. (Ethics and aesthetics are one and the same.)" (6.421) The specific reason given in this context for this conclusion is that so-called ethical propositions or laws have no consequences in the experiential world. Thus such utterances, like those about the self, reflect the character of the limits of our world--our perspective or horizons--rather than something in the world. "The world of the happy man is a different one from that of the unhappy man" (6.43).

Further, the overall view Wittgenstein is proposing eliminates religious utterances about life after death and God's activity in the world from the realm of meaningful discourse because their subject matter lies outside the experiential world, outside space and time (6.4312). "God does not reveal himself in the world" (6.432). There can be nothing "mystical" in the world because only answerable questions can be formed within the structure of thought (6.5). The "mystical", by definition, is concerned with things that cannot be got at through thought and facts, so it cannot be expressed by them; which means it cannot be expressed at all.

We feel that even when all possible scientific questions have been answered, the problems of life remain completely untouched. Of course there are then no questions left, and this itself is the answer.
The solution of the problem of life is

seen in the vanishing of the problem.
(6.52 and 6.521)

Thus Wittgenstein concludes, as did Kant, that the only "correct" method of doing philosophy is to say, along with everyone else, nothing except the propositions of science, and when someone tries to utter a metaphysical statement explain to him that such matters lie outside the realm of meaningful discourse because they seek to answer questions that are unaskable (6.53). "There are, indeed, things that cannot be put into words" (6.522)..."What we cannot speak about we must consign to silence" (7). Such things, though unsayable, "make themselves manifest" (6.522). We have, then, two realms, the meaningful (empirical) and the unsayable (mystical). They are separated by the thin line of logic as it permeates thought and language. The philosopher's function is to walk this line and keep people from confusing the two realms.

All of which brings us back to the issue which was postponed several times earlier on, and one which Wittgenstein himself addresses head-on on the last page of the _Tractatus_. Just what is the status of propositions which express the relationship between the factual realm and the value realm, namely those propositions of logic in general (which are supposed to "manifest" themselves while being, strictly speaking, "unutterable") and those of Wittgenstein's _Tractatus_, in particular? Is there not some sense in which these statements are meaningful, a sense other than the empirical sense? If not, how have they been understood?

Wittgenstein's answer to this query involves yet another use of the "outside" or "beyond" metaphor. He says:

> My propositions serve as elucidations
> in the following way:  anyone who under-
> stands me eventually recognizes them as
> nonsensical, when he has used them--as
> steps--to climb up beyond them.  (He
> must, so to speak, throw away the ladder
> after he has climbed up it. (6.54)

In a word,he clearly says that his propositions do not conform to his own definition of
meaningful discourse and thus can only be classified as nonsensical.  The "kicker" is that they
are to be so classified after they have been
understood.  Wittgenstein's propositions are to
be used as steps and rungs of a ladder which
carry one "beyond" the confines of the limits of
language and thought.  Once having arrived at
this transcendent position, once having understood
the sense of these nonempirical utterances, we
can classify them as senseless and pretend we
never used them.

The problem is, of course, that according
to Wittgenstein's overall position there is no
place to stand "outside" the realm of the empirical world, and thus we must be standing on the
top rung of the ladder provided by his propositions when we throw the ladder away.  In other
words, either (1) his propositions have sense,
in which case his criterion for meaningful utterances is too narrow and we do not need to--
indeed, cannot--throw them away.  Or (2) his
propositions do not have sense and we cannot begin climbing at all.  To put it differently, the
metaphors of logical space and logical pictures
systematically eliminate the possibility of an
"outside", and yet such an "Archemedian point"
is necessary to the development of these metaphors.

## 6.  Summary and Conclusion

There are a number of points that need to
be summarized before moving to a consideration
of Wittgenstein's later work.  Quite obviously
the dominant and common element in the major
metaphors of the Tractatus is spatiality.  Beginning with the notions of "logical space" and
"logical pictures" on down through the correlative concepts of "logical limit", "logical network", and "outside", spatial relationships are
always at the fore.  This central characteristic
provides the point of integration for understanding the Tractatus as a whole, and yet to
my knowledge its importance has gone largely
unmentioned in the literature on the work.  The
extent to which it is acknowledged is usually
limited to pointing out that the Tractatus is
based on a mathematical or geometric model which
may have grown out of his work with Russell.
There are qualities and limitations inherent
within spatial metaphors and which need unpacking.  Although most of this unpacking will be
postponed until later, there are several points
that can be delineated at this time.

To be more specific, the root metaphor of
the Tractatus is not simply spatiality, but is
what might be called "visual space".  That is
to say, the point of view is invariably that of
how things would be seen to relate to one another.  This theme is particularly well focused
in the picture theory of meaning with its emphasis on the mirroring of the common logical
form between facts and propositions.  Moreover,
Wittgenstein's treatment of logical space is in
terms of points in relation to one another as
seen by an observer, rather than from the perspective of the points themselves.  In other
words, the stress is not on being at a point

93

but upon <u>visualizing</u> a point's position in space in relation to other points, all of which are located over-against the viewer. The same holds true for such notions as logical limit, logical network, and being outside the world. For in each case the phenomenon in question is described from a position which lies outside the phenomenon itself.

It is, of course, hardly surprising to encounter this visual-spatial metaphor at this juncture in the history of philosophy, since it has played a major, if not <u>the</u> major, role in epistemological concerns since Plato. Ever since Plato introduced his cave allegory and defined the mind as "the eye of the soul" philosophers have been prone to base their epistemological models on vision, defining "knowing" in terms of "seeing" and "error" in terms of visual illusion and hallucination. The visual metaphor has become especially prevalent in modern times, expressing itself in such notions as "clear and distinct" knowledge, "the natural light of reason", "intuitive insight", and "knowledge by acquaintance". Anyone familiar with philosophic literature will acknowledge the dominance of examples dealing with knowing and error in terms of correct and incorrect vision. In some ways this is an understandable pattern, since as humans we do tend to rely more heavily on our sense of sight. Nevertheless it can be argued that the dominance of the visual-spatial metaphor has distorted our understanding of the knowing experience and that an exploration of metaphors rooted in the other senses, especially those of hearing, touching, and moving, would prove most helpful. This in fact is one way to characterize the posture of the later Wittgenstein, as will become apparent further on.

Yet another important characteristic of this visual space model is its <u>static</u> quality. Throughout Wittgenstein's discussion of "logical space", <u>et al</u>, there is not the slightest indication of any movement, change, or interaction among the constituents. Everything has its place, whether in the realm of the actual or in the realm of the possible, and the logical form of this place is reflected in language, not in the act of speaking but in static propositions. It is a world of cold, crystaline purity structured by a logic which can deal only with being (how things <u>are</u>), not with becoming (how things <u>change</u>). Here again one can acknowledge both strengths and weaknesses. The comprehensive scope and integrating power of the spatial model are obvious. Nevertheless, Wittgenstein came to feel that the price that is paid for this scope and power is exorbitant, since it invariably yields a distorted understanding of both the world and language. These considerations will be the concern of the next chapter.

One final matter before moving on. As was mentioned earlier, there is no justification offered within the <u>Tractatus</u> for the use of the spatial metaphor. It provides, rather, the framework, or to borrow Wittgenstein's term, the "scaffolding" within which the doctrines of the <u>Tractatus</u> are laid out. The problem here is similar to that inherent in the picture theory, namely that a picture cannot be both a picture of a state of affairs and a picture of the fact that it is such a picture. Or at a deeper level, Wittgenstein cannot <u>say</u> both that language pictures reality and that this cannot be <u>said</u>. The question is, can a philosophical position be presented without providing a justification for the ground upon which it is based? Traditionally to do so has been considered a serious deficiency. On the other hand, it is possible to argue that it is precisely at this point that Wittgenstein has made his most important contribution to philosophy. For in both his early and later work the justification for the overall position is grounded in the employment of certain key metaphors which in the traditional sense of the word remain unjustified. An effort will be made in Part Three to ascertain more carefully the character and significance of this procedure.

The literature on the role of metaphor in the Tractatus is almost non-existent. Accounts of the picture theory occasionally make brief mention of it. See, for example, Erik Stenius' Wittgenstein's Tractatus (Oxford:  Blackwell, 1960), G.E.M. Anscomb's An Introduction To Wittgenstein's Tractatus (New York:  Harper, 1963, and George Pitcher's The Philosophy of Wittgenstein (Englewood Cliffs:  Prentice-Hall, 1964). It is especially surprising that Max Black, who has done important work on the significance of metaphor (cf. his Models and Metaphors, Ithaca:  Cornell University Press, 1959), has only this to say in his otherwise highly helpful Companion to Wittgenstein's Tractatus (Ithaca:  Cornell University Press, 1964):

> Of strict argument, there is very little in the book, Wittgenstein occasionally uses informal argument to clinch a point, but his main insights are presented dogmatically. A sympathetic response calls for a willing suspension of disbelief in the visual metaphors ('pictures' Wittgenstein later called them) which lend those insights their force and their support. (p. 3)

# Chapter Five

--Metaphors in The <u>Philosophical Investigations</u>--

In <u>Philosophical Investigations</u> Wittgenstein uses a far greater number of analogical
and/or metaphorical expressions than he does in
the <u>Tractatus</u>. To be sure, the former is a
much larger work, but the increase is far more
significant than the comparative sizes of the
books would suggest. The ramifications of this
increase will be examined later on. Suffice it
to say at this point that it will be necessary
to limit the scope of this chapter to those
metaphorical expressions which carry the most
freight in the development of Wittgenstein's
overall position.

1. Language-Games (<u>Sprachspiele</u>)

This is undoubtedly the most widely known
of all of Wittgenstein's notions. It is introduced early (#7, #23, and #130) and is given
three separate but related uses at the outset.

> "We can also think of the whole process
> of using words in (2) as one of those
> games by means of which children learn
> their native language. I will call these
> games "language-games" and will sometimes
> speak of a primitive language as a lan-
> guage-game.
> And the processes of naming the stones
> and of repeating words after someone
> might also be called language-games.
> Think of much of the use of words in

games like ring-a-ring-a-roses.
    I shall also call the whole, con-
sisting of language and the actions
into which it is woven the "language-
game"." (#7)

First off, Wittgenstein uses it to speak of
the "primitive languages" he invents by way of
illustrating the nature and shortcomings of the
picture theory of meaning (#7).  He does not
argue that the picture theory is entirely inadequate, only that it hardly does justice to the
multifarious character of language.  Words sometimes function as names, and statements sometimes function as pictures of states of affairs.
But such cases are better thought of as specific
("primitive") language-games within the broader
fabric of language as a whole (#2, #3).  Thus
both the view espoused by Augustine (#1) and
that layed out in the Tractatus (#23) are limited and misleading as models for coming to grips
with the nature of language in general.

Secondly, Wittgenstein sometimes uses the
term 'language-game' to refer to the simple
games that children play when learning the names
of things or when enjoying "nonsense" games and
singing catches.  The point of these first two
uses of the notion is not to offer them as the
"building blocks" out of which more complex
linguistic usages may be seen as being constructed.

    "Our clear and simple language-games
    are not preparatory studies for a
    future regularization of language--as
    it were first approximation, ignoring
    friction and air-resistance.  The lan-
    guage-games are rather set up as objects
    of comparison which are meant to throw
    light on the facts of our language by

way not only of similarities, but also of dissimilarities." (#130)

Thirdly, Wittgenstein most frequently speaks of the fabric comprised of human speech and human action as a language-game. In these cases he is speaking of specific "regions" within the total network of a natural language, which when taken together can be said to make up linguistic reality, or more generally to make up a "form of life" (#19). These linguistic "sub-sets" overlap and evolve in relation to various forms of human behavior, with no sharp boundaries between them.

The primary thrust of this Wittgenstein's major use of the language-game metaphor is to call attention to the fact that speaking is a kind of doing--not only in the sense of making noises, etc. but more significantly in the sense that utterances are made by persons in concrete contexts for certain purposes. "Words are also deeds" (#546). It was this aspect of Wittgenstein's work that J.L. Austin developed in his How to Do Things With Words. Perhaps the following paragraph is Wittgenstein's most succinct statement of his insight:

> "But how many kinds of sentence are there? Say assertion, question, and command?--There are countless kinds: countless different kinds of use of what we call 'symbols', 'words', 'sentences'. And this multiplicity is not something fixed, given once for all; but new types of language, new language-games, as we may say, come into existence, and others become obsolete and get forgotten. (We can get a rough picture of this from the changes in mathematics.) Here the term

99

'language-game' is meant to bring into
prominence the fact that the speaking
of language is part of an activity, or
of a form of life.
Review the multiplicity of language-
games in the following examples, and
in others:
Giving orders, and obeying them--
Describing the appearance of an object,
or giving its measurements--
Constructing an object from a descrip-
tion (a drawing)--
Reporting an event--
Speculating about an event--
Forming and testing a hypothesis--
Presenting the results of an experiment
in tables and diagrams--
Making up a story; and reading it--
Play-acting--
Singing catches--
Guessing riddles--
Making a joke; telling it--
Solving a problem in practical arithmetic--
Translating from one language into another--
Asking, thanking, cursing, greeting,
praying.
--It is interesting to compare the multi-
plicity of the tools in language and of
the ways they are used, the multiplicity
of kinds of word and sentence, with what
logicians have said about the structure
of language.
(Including the author of the Tractatus
Logico-Philosophicus.)" (#23)

Thus language-games provide the dynamic context within which specific utterances carry
meaning, while they themselves find their meaning within the framework provided by a form of
life.  We shall return to this latter notion
later on in the chapter.  As becomes clear from

Wittgenstein's discussion of the relation between linguistic rules and meaning (e.g. #54), language-games are thought of as comprised of a constantly evolving set of conventions which are always only applicable to a greater or lesser degree. The burden of the metaphor is the notion of linguistic _activity_ and not the suggestion that language follows a strict set of rules. Moreover, it is also clear from Wittgenstein's use of this language-game metaphor that he in no sense intends to imply any degree of triviality by the term 'game'. The stress is on the social interaction of linguistic expression.

One other aspect of this metaphor needs to be unpacked. In conjoining speech and action together in the way he does, Wittgenstein constructs serious inroads into the modern dogma that language and behavior are essentially unrelated, the former being optional while the latter is essentially real. Not only is speech now seen as an important aspect of behavior, and thus of reality, but the dynamic relation between it and the world (behavior plus things) is seen as symbiotic in character. The world as we know it is dependent to a large degree on the language we use to engage it, even as our use of speech is a result of our efforts to engage the world.

> "So you are saying that human agreement decides what is true and what is false?" --It is what human beings _say_ that is true and false; and they agree in the _language_ they use. That is not agreement in opinions but in form of life. If language is to be a means of communication there must be agreement not only in definition but also (queer as this may sound) in judgments. This seems to abolish logic, but does not

do so.--It is one thing to describe
methods of measurement, and another
to obtain and state results of measurement.  But what we call 'measuring'
is partly determined by a certain constancy in results of measurement."
(#241, 242)


2.  Use and Function (<u>Gebrauch</u> <u>und</u> <u>Funktion</u>)

        Whether or not Wittgenstein's suggestion
that meaning is mediated by use involves a metaphorical employment of the term 'use' (and in
some passages 'function') is perhaps open for
debate.  Be that as it may, it is indisputable
that in the course of developing this point of
view he makes use of a number of metaphors
anchored in the notion of instrumentation.
These metaphors are offered as analogies for
illuminating the relation between language and
meaning, and as such they are crucial to Wittgenstein's overall position.

        One such metaphor is that of the tool.
Wittgenstein often sets up a parallel between
language and the social world on the one hand
and tools and the physical world on the other.
As tools are used to accomplish specific tasks
in the physical world, so speech is used to get
certain jobs done in the social world.  The
"meaning" of the tool is revealed in and by its
function.  The same is said to hold true for the
meaning of various utterances.

        "Think of the tools in a tool-box:
        there is a hammer, pliers, a saw, a
        screw-driver, a rule, a glue-pot,
        nails and screws.--The functions of
        words are as diverse as the functions
        of these objects.  (And in both cases

102

there are similarities.)
Of course, what confuses us is the
uniform appearance of words when we
hear them spoken or meet them in
script and print. For their <u>appli-
cation</u> is not presented to us so
clearly. Especially not, when we are
doing philosophy!" (#11)

In a later context Wittgenstein is dealing
with the problem of the meaning of talk about
mental experience. As part of his overall argument against viewing such talk as referring to
private, "spiritual" entities--a view which
leads to many traditional and serious difficul-
ties--Wittgenstein maintains that the meaning of
statements about mental experience is not to be
found in mysterious, inner referents, but rather
in the use to which these statements are put in
social contexts. He concludes by advising:
"Look at the sentence as an instrument, and at
its sense as its employment [Verwendung]"
(#421 cf. also #569).

In another, earlier, passage Wittgenstein
shifts the image slightly by calling to mind the
"logic" of handles:

"It is like looking into the cabin of
a locomotive. We see handles all looking more or less alike. (Naturally,
since they are all supposed to be
handled.) But one is the handle of a
crank which can be moved continuously
(it regulates the opening of a valve);
another is the handle of a switch, which
has only two effective positions, it is
either off or on; a third is the handle
of a brake-lever, the harder one pulls
on it, the harder it brakes; a fourth,
the handle of a pump: it has an effect

103

only so long as it is moved to and
fro." (#12)

Here again the notion of meaning is related to
that of function, and not to surface similarity.

Yet another instrumentation metaphor em-
ployed in <u>Philosophical</u> <u>Investigations</u> is that
of games in general and the game of chess in
particular. In addition to using the concept
of 'game' to cast light on the relation between
rules and meaning in language (#83), Wittgenstein also uses it to suggest that meaning is
more functional than definitional: "The question 'What is a word really?' is analogous to
'What is a piece of chess?'" (#108). And further: "Let us say that the meaning of a piece
is its role in the game" (#563). Once again the
question of the meaning of talk about mental
experiences (this time the language-game involving terms like 'think') is treated as analogous to the question of the meaning of specific
moves in chess.

"In order to get clear about the
meaning of the word 'think' we
watch ourselves while we think:
what we observe will be what the
word means!--But this concept is
not used like that. (It would be
as if without knowing how to play
chess, I were to try and make out
what the word 'mate' meant by close
observation of the last move of some
game of chess.)" (#316)

In the course of his discussion of the sense
in which those entities referred to by a common
term can be said to possess some immutable characteristic in common, Wittgenstein introduces

the metaphor of "family resemblance" (#66-71).
Against those who would argue that the common
use of the term 'game', for instance, necessarily
implies a single characteristic shared by all
games, Wittgenstein claims that this move is
superfluous. For we neither originally learn how
to use the term 'game' by being given such a
characteristic, nor do we call one to mind whenever we employ the term. Indeed, when pressed
we cannot even discover such a characteristic.
Rather, he suggests, the referrents of the term
'game' are related by a series of overlapping
characteristics in the same way that members of
a family can be said to resemble one another
even though they do not all share one particular
feature. A, B, and C may have similar eyes, while
B, C, and D have similar noses, yet A, C, and D
have similar hair, etc. The notion of family
resemblance is offered as a replacement for that
of common or universal characteristic. Moreover,
it is argued that the sort of exactitude which
is said to be lost by such a substitution is
itself an unnecessary requirement. Use and
function are logically prior to exact definition.

> "To repeat, we can draw a boundary--
> for a special purpose. Does it take
> that to make the concept usable? Not
> at all! (Except for that special
> purpose.) No more than it took the
> definition: 1 pace = 75 cm. to make
> the measure of length 'one pace' usable.
> And if you want to say 'But still, be-
> fore that it wasn't an exact measure',
> then I reply: very well, it was an
> inexact one.--Though you still owe
> me a definition of exactness. (#69)
> 'But if the concept 'game' is uncir-
> cumscribed like that, you don't really

know what you mean by a 'game'.'--When
I give the description: 'The ground
was quite covered with plants'--do you
want to say I don't know what I am talking about until I can give a definition
of a plant?" (#70)

One last "use and function" metaphor bears
mentioning. While developing his idea that
meaning is a function of use, Wittgenstein
suggests that one might profitably compare
linguistic meaning with monetary value:

"You say:  the point isn't the word,
but its meaning, and you think of the
meaning as a thing of the same kind as
the word, though also different from the
word. Here the word, there the meaning.
The money, and the cow that you can buy
with it. (But contrast:  money, and
its use.)" (#120)

Rather than think of words as money and meaning
as the object(s) we can buy with it, he is
asking that we think of words as money and
meaning as the use we make of it. For we can buy
more than one kind of thing with money, and even
this varies from place to place and time to time.
Moreover, we do other things with money, such as
exchange it, save it, and lend it. Thus meaning
is more akin to the value of money than it is to
the objects it buys. Value can be determined
neither by scrutinizing the money itself nor by
examining the objects. It can only be determined by using the money in a variety of contexts. The same holds true for meaning.

Elsewhere, while discussing the possibility
of a "private language", Wittgenstein uses the
money metaphor again. He argues that while one
can talk to himself no social tasks are accomplished by such speech and thus it has no ling-

uistic meaning. Moreover, since the speaker and
hearer are the same person whatever is said must
be accepted--and this is the same as saying that
nothing is accepted (#258). Then he says:

> "Why can't my right hand give my
> left hand money?--May right hand can
> put it into my left hand. My right
> hand can write a deed of gift and my
> left hand a receipt.--But the further
> practical consequences would not be
> those of a gift. When the left hand has
> taken the money from the right, etc.,
> we shall ask: 'Well, and what of it?'
> And the same could be asked if a person
> had given himself a private definition
> of a word; I mean, if he has said the
> word to himself and at the same time
> has directed his attention to a
> sensation." (#268)

## 3. Walking (Gehen)

There is a large number of metaphors in the
Investigations having to do with getting around
and/or finding one's way. Sometimes the concern is directional--which path to take--and
other times it is kinesthetic--getting from one
place to another. I shall treat this rather
diverse group of metaphors as sharing family
resemblances because it is a helpful way of
organizing certain important notions.

Early on in the Investigations (#18) Wittgenstein likens ordinary language to an ancient
city, with irregular architecture and winding
streets. His concern at this point is to present the open-ended quality of language in such
a manner as to show that being open-ended in no
way renders language "incomplete".

"Do not be troubled by the fact that
languages (2) and (8) consist only of
orders.  If you want to say that this
shows them to be incomplete, ask yourself whether our language is complete;
--whether it was so before the symbolism
of chemistry and the notation of the
infinitesimal calculus were incorporated in it; for these are, so to speak,
suburbs of our language.  (And how many
houses or streets does it take before a
town begins to be a town?)  Our language can be seen as an ancient city:  a
maze of little streets and squares, of
old and new houses, and of houses with
additions from various periods; and this
surrounded by a multitude of new boroughs
with straight regular streets and uniform houses." (#18)

In some ways this metaphor may be thought
of as pivotal in delineating the difference
between the views of language in the Tractatus
and the Investigations.  In the latter language is viewed as an ancient city (ordinary
language) with its complexities and irregular-
ities surrounded by modern well laid out suburbs (various scientific languages).  These
suburbs came into being after and depend for
their ongoing life upon the ancient city, and
thus cannot be used as the standard against
which to judge it.  In the Tractatus, on the
other hand, language is viewed as a rigidly
laid-out compound within the teaming jungles
of nonsense.  Meaning can only exist within the
limits of this compound, it is the only standard there is.  In the world of the Investigations ordinary language is alright as it is and
the philosopher's task is to help people (especially theoreticians) find their way about.

In the world of the <u>Tractatus</u> ordinary language is often muddled, in need of clarification, and the philosopher's task is to regulate speech by reminding people of what can and cannot be said.

This same theme is introduced in #203 where Wittgenstein says: "Language is a labyrinth of paths. You approach from <u>one</u> side and know your way about; you approach the same place from another side and no longer know your way about." It is in this context that his view of philosophy as a kind of therapy whereby we are relieved of certain "mental cramps" is best understood (#255). Showing "the fly the way out of the fly bottle" (#309) also implies an "I don't know my way about" (#123) motif. The main point of all of these metaphors is to reveal the fact that the use of language is an activity, like walking, in which we often find ourselves either making unhappy moves or unable to make the next move. Philosophy can help us resolve these puzzles, "not by giving new information, but by arranging what we have always known. Philosophy is a battle against the bewitchment of our intelligence by means of language" (#109). It helps us "know how to go on" (#179-180).

In other contexts Wittgenstein speaks of the place of rules in learning and using language in terms of signposts and arrows (#85-86). In finding our way walking through the country side we often make use of signs as directional indicators. But it ought to be remembered: that: (1) the signs themselves are essentially vague, for they do not specify whether one is to take the path, the road, or go cross-country, nor do they always indicate their range of application (to the next corner, the next county, or completely around the globe); and (2) they depend for their being understood upon a knowledge of how to read arrows, which itself cannot be

learned exclusively through the use of arrows.
The point here is not to criticize travel signs
and/or linguistic rules, but rather to indicate
that complete precision is neither sufficient
nor necessary to the business of getting around.

A different dimension of the walking metaphor is brought out when Wittgenstein deals with
the relation between precision and meaning in
terms of the difference between walking on ice
and walking on rough ground (#107). He maintains that the attempt to impose the standards
of logic on the expressions of ordinary language, as he himself had proposed in the _Tracta-
tus_, is to forget that the latter are logically
prior to the former. In fact, they are, in
Strawson's terms, "logically primitive" in relation to all other forms of linguistic expression.
To place undue premium on precision is to ignore
the law of diminishing returns. For the logical
empiricist criterion of meaning results in making it impossible for us to accomplish many of
the linguistic tasks essential to our way of
being in the world. As Wittgenstein so powerfully puts it:

> "The more narrowly we examine actual
> language, the sharper becomes the con-
> flict between it and our requirement.
> (For the crystal-line purity of logic
> was, of course, not a _result of inves-
> tigation_: it was a requirement.) The
> conflict becomes intolerable; the re-
> quirement is now in danger of becoming
> empty.--We have got on to slippery ice
> where there is no friction and so in a
> certain sense the conditions are ideal,
> but also, just because of that, we are
> unable to walk. We want to walk:  so
> we need _friction_. Back to the rough
> ground!" (#107)

# 4. Knowing As Doing (Wissen als Anwendung)

In order to make a case against the traditional epistemological position that knowing (and/or understanding) is a private mental act or passive state of consciousness, Wittgenstein employs a number of metaphors which display the public and active character of knowing. Although he uses these metaphors in widely separated contexts and although they may at first glance seem disparate, I think grouping them together in this way brings out an important and often overlooked emphasis in the Investigations.

In paragraphs #75-78 Wittgenstein addresses the relationship between knowing, saying and showing. He maintains that it is not only possible but common for us to "know more than we can say" and that this knowledge is not in any way "hidden", but rather it displays itself in the way we interact with the environment context, including the relevant language-game(s). He says:

> "What does it mean to know what a game is? What does it mean, to know it and not to be able to say it? Is this knowledge somehow equivalent to an unformulated definition? So that if it were formulated I should be able to recognize it as the expression of my knowledge? Isn't my knowledge, my concept of a game, completely expressed in the explanations that I could give? That is, in my describing examples of various kinds of game; showing how all sorts of other games can be constructed on the analogy of these; saying that I should scarcely include this or this among

games; and so on." (#75).
"Compare knowing and saying:
    how many feet high Mont Blanc is--
    how the word "game" is used--
    how a clarinet sounds.
If you are surprised that one can know
something and not be able to say it,
you are perhaps thinking of a case like
the first. Certainly not of one like
the third." (#78)

Later on in the Investigations (#146-155)
Wittgenstein focuses on the relationship between
knowledge and application. Against the traditional dichotomy between knowing something and
applying it, Wittgenstein suggests an alternative
view wherein the application alone becomes the
defining characteristic of knowledge since it is
the application alone which serves as the justification for the claim to know. There are not
two distinct sets of criteria, one for knowing
something and another for applying it. If a
person claims to know and consistently fails in
the application we deny the claim--and vice
versa (#149-152). Moreover, we often use such
phrases as "now I know..." and "Now I understand..." as signals rather than as a descriptions of mental states or private events (cf.
#179-180). Wittgenstein makes these observa-
tions:

    "The grammar of the word "knows" is
    evidently closely related to that of
    "can", "is able to". But also closely
    related to that of "understands".
    ('Mastery' of a technique,)" (#150)
    "But there is also this use of the
    word "to know": we say 'Now I know!'
    --and similarly 'Now I can do it!' and
    'Now I understand!'" (#151)

"Suppose it were asked: 'When do you know
how to play chess? All the time? or just
while you are making a move? And the whole
of chess during each move?--How queer that
knowing how to play chess should take such
a short time, and a game so much longer!"
(#151b)

Wittgenstein continues his case against knowing and understanding being thought of as names
for states and processes by developing a parallel with music. In #332 he likens the relation
between understanding and language to that between musical expression and the notes of a particular tune. One can say words without understanding and one can sing a tune without expression. But one cannot have the understanding
apart from the words anymore than one can have
the expressions apart from the tune. In each
case the latter is the vehicle of the former.
(cf. #320). Here again understanding or knowing
is presented as a kind of doing, as the skill of
discerning meaning as it is mediated in and
through public behavior, which displays itself
in the way a person interacts with the context.

This parallel between language and music is
brought up again in #527. One's claim to understand a piece of music is not justified by being
explained in terms of something else, some non-
musical phenomenon such as intuition or private
cognitive accomplishments. Rather it is justified in terms of factors inherent within the
piece of music itself. What one knows displays
itself, not in a definition or a formula, but
in dialogue with other prehenders about the
piece. In the same way, one's understanding of
an utterance or situation is not justified by
referring to some private experience, but by
dealing with and responding to it appropriately.

"Understanding a sentence is much more akin to understanding a theme in music than one may think. What I mean is that understanding a sentence lies nearer than one thinks to what is ordinarily called understanding a musical theme. Why is just _this_ the pattern of variation in loudness and tempo? One would like to say 'Because I know what it's all about.' But what is it all about? I should not be able to say. In order to 'explain' I could only compare it with something else which has the same rhythm (I mean the same pattern). (One says 'Don't you see, this is as if a conclusion were being drawn' or 'This is as it were a parenthesis', etc. How does one justify such comparisons?--There are very different kinds of justification here.)" (#527)

In section XI of Part Two of _Investigations_ Wittgenstein offers two other metaphors for understanding as a kind of doing. The first is that of "noticing an aspect", seeing a phenomenon in a particular way or from a particular perspective ("seeing as..."), and it is developed from page 193 to page 215. After presenting a number of examples of what he calls "two uses of the word 'see'" - two dimensional cubes, duck-rabbits, double-crosses, and the like - Wittgenstein concludes that "seeing as..." is like seeing, yet significantly different (p.197), and like interpretation, but very unlike it as well (p. 212). One of the main reasons for the differences in each case is that "seeing as..." can be a result of volition while perception and interpretation cannot. In the former case: "Seeing an aspect and imagining are subject to the will. There is such an order as 'Imagine this', and also: 'Now see the figure like this'; but not: 'Now see this leaf green'" (p. 213). In the latter case: "Do I really see something different each time, or do I only interpret what I see in a different way? I am inclined to say the former. But why?--to interpret is to think, to do something; seeing is a state: (p. 212). So, for Wittgenstein, "seeing as..." lies half way between simple perception and interpretation; it is more active than the former and less so than the latter.

The point of this analysis is to use "seeing as..." or "noticing an aspect" as a metaphor for grasping the relationship between understanding and language. Understanding, like "seeing as..." is more than merely being exposed to the verbal data but less than a full-scale, conscious inter-pretation of that data. Thus the "more" of understanding is not something experienced in addition to the data, such as a mental picture or interpretation, but something grasped and displayed in interaction with the data in a concrete context.

"The importance of this concept lies in the connexion between the concepts of 'seeing an aspect' and 'experiencing the meaning of a word'. For we want to ask 'What would you be missing if you did not experience the meaning of a word?'...You can say the word 'March' to yourself and mean it at one time as an imperative at another as the name of a month. And now say 'March!'--and then 'March no further!'--Does the same ex-perience accompany the word both times-- are you sure?" (pp. 214-215)

The second metaphor introduced in this section of the _Investigations_ (pp. 227-228) is that of "imponderable evidence". Once again the context is that of the justification of knowledge claims, this time of claims concerning such things as the genuineness of expressions of feelings. While there is less agreement about such claims than we often would like, and while the criteria for judging such claims cannot be articulated fully, nevertheless there is such a thing as "expert judgment" in these areas and certain persons can rightly be said to "know" about such matters. This knowledge is acquired through experiential exposure and apprenticeship and it is made manifest in the performance of correct judgments (p. 227). In addition, this knowledge can be communicated to others and thus justified by the use of "imponderable evidence" (_unwagbare evidenz_). This sort of evidence may be "unweighable" in a quantitative sense, but it still has its appropriate effect epistemologically. Moreover, it is revealed in various forms of behavior.

> "It is certainly possible to be convinced by evidence that someone is in such-and-such a state of mind, that, for instance, he is not pretending. But 'evidence' here includes 'imponderable' evidence.
>
> The question is:  what does imponderable evidence _accomplish_? Suppose there were imponderable evidence for the chemical (internal) structure of a substance, still it would have to prove itself to be evidence by certain consequences which _can_ be weighed.
> (Imponderable evidence might convince someone that a picture was a genuine... But it is _possible_ for this to be proved

116

right by documentary evidence as well.)
Imponderable evidence includes subtle-
ties of glance, of gesture, of tone.
I may recognize a genuine loving look,
distinguish it from a pretended one
(and here there can, of course, be a
'ponderable' confirmation of my judgment). But I may be quite incapable
of describing the difference. And this
not because the languages I know have
no words for it. For why not introduce new words? --If I were a very
talented painter I might conceivably
represent the genuine and the simulated glance in pictures.

Ask yourself: How does a man learn to
get a 'nose' for something? And how
can this nose be used?" (p. 228)


## 5. Bedrock

There is one other major metaphor used by
Wittgenstein in the Investigations, one which
integrates nearly all of the others discussed on
the foregoing pages. In fact, it can be said to
lie at the very basis of all of them. This
metaphor is that of "bedrock", and it is introduced most forcefully in #217 where Wittgenstein
is discussing the justification of the behavior
patterns which express the human way of integrating language and reality. With specific
references to the justification of rule-follow-
ing behaviour Wittgenstein says:

"'How am I able to obey a rule?'--if
this is not a question about causes, then
it is about the justification for my following the rule in the way I do.

117

If I have exhausted the justifications
I have reached bedrock, and my spade is
turned. Then I am inclined to say:
'This is simply what I do.'" (#217)

Another way to put this is to question the
modern dogma that every behavioral move, especially in what is called rational analysis,
must be justified or explained in terms of something else. As Wittgenstein says in #485, if
justification did not come to an end "it would
not be justification." To suppose that every
move can and must be explained in terms of another is to undercut the whole notion of explanation. For one would never be justified in
making _any_ move until he had made _all_ of them,
since there would be either an infinite number
of moves or a finite number arranged in a vicious circle. There would, in short, be no
place to begin.

"Our mistake is to look for an explanation where we ought to look at
what happens as a 'proto-phenomenon'.
That is, where we ought to have said:
This language-game is played. (#654)
"The question is not one of explaining a language-game by means of our
experiences, but of noting a language-
game." (#655)

The notion of bedrock, or "proto-phenomenon"
avoids the above difficulty by avoiding both the
infinite regress and the vicious circle. It
provides an end point in which justifications
can come to rest and a place from which they can
begin. To put the matter in Kurt Gödel's terms,
no symbolic system (not even and perhaps especially not the fabric of ordinary, natural
language) can be exhaustively explained in terms
of itself. At some point one must both begin

and end. In Wittgenstein's view this point is not arbitrary in the case of our natural language, since it is the point at which our speech and our actions conjoin. This conjunction of language and action within the concrete contexts provided by physical and social reality constitutes the human way-of-being-in-the-world, what Wittgenstein calls the human "form of life" (cf. p. 226).

"'So you are saying that human agreement decides what is true and what is false?' --It is what human beings say that is true and false; and they agree in the language they use. That is not agreement in opinions but in form of life." (#241)
"If language is to be a means of communication there must be agreement not only in definitions but also (queer as this may sound) in judgments. This seems to abolish logic, but does not do so.-- It is one thing to describe methods of measurement, and another to obtain and state results of measurement. But what we call 'measuring' is partly determined by a certain constancy in results of measurement." (#242)

In this way Wittgenstein employs the "bedrock" metaphor to cast light on the nature of justification in relation to our activity in the world. "What people accept as justification --is shown by how they think and live" (#325). "What we are supplying are really remarks on the natural history of human beings..."(#415). Thus it can be seen that the metaphor of bedrock also fits within the family of metaphors which portray knowing as a kind of doing.

119

## 6. Summary and Conclusion

There are a number of features exhibited in varying degrees of commonality by the metaphors discussed in this chapter. Perhaps the most obvious is that of action. Language-games, use and function, finding one's way about, and knowing as a kind of doing--these notions all consist of kinesthetic involvement. Language itself is depicted as being alive, and our relation to it and to the world is presented as dynamic and symbiotic in character. The dominant stress is on the use of muscles, from facial expressions, gestures, and intonations to grasping handles, moving chess pieces, and walking around.

The contrast that exists between the metaphors used in the Investigations and those used in the Tractatus is diametrical and striking. In fact, it is almost impossible to over-emphasize the importance of this contrast. It lies at the very basis of the difference between Wittgenstein's early and later work, and in addition it constitutes the line of demarcation between logical empiricism and ordinary language analysis as ways of doing philosophy. In spite of its pivotal role, however, this difference in kinds of metaphors used has to my knowledge never been noted in any of the literature published about Wittgenstein. Attention will be given to unpacking the significance of this difference in Chapter Eight. It is sufficient at this juncture to note that while the world of the Tractatus is spatial, static, and visual in character, the world of the Investigations is kinesthetic, active, and tactile. In the former, language is comprised of "names" and "mental pictures" whereas in the latter it consists of "tools" and "deeds".

Another family likeness amongst these metaphors is that in some way or other they involve the notion of purpose.  Games, tasks, journies, and knowing call our attention to the fact that the human form of life is focused in intentionality.  It is this quality which provides the contextual character of our existence, wherein we attend _from_ some elements in the world and life _to_ others.  Thus the main metaphors of the _Investigations_ relate language to life in an integral fashion.  Here again we see clearly the difference between the early and later work of Wittgenstein.  For in the _Tractatus_ language is treated, by means of the main metaphors, as parallel to the world and life but essentially unrelated to it.  Mirroring bears a dispensible connection with the world, while purposeful activity is inextricably bound up with it.

A third feature worth mentioning is that of _community_.  The metaphors of the _Investigations_ are embedded in the social character of human existence.  Games, tools, paths, cities, and judgments can only exist within a social matrix.  Here the dynamic quality of Wittgenstein's metaphors comes to the fore.  The give-and-take aspect of human interaction is emphasized as the foundation of language.  In addition, the social dimension of the human form of life provides both poles of linguistic activity, convention and innovation.  Wittgenstein's model of language as open-textured fits smoothly into what we know about the nature of social reality, for it is seen to function within flexible boundaries as conserved and modified by human interaction.  That this is not the case with the view of language mediated by the metaphors of the _Tractatus_ should be clear.  They convey a model of language which is at best the result of a single observer and even borders on being completely devoid of any human quality whatsoever.  To put it

121

differently, the world of the _Tractatus_, is indeed atomistic and solipsistic.

And this brings up a final observation. There is a sense in which the metaphors of the _Investigations_ display the relation amongst language, the world, and human behavior from the inside. That is to say, the perspective is not, as in the _Tractatus_, that of an observer describing this relationship objectively from a distance. Rather, it is the perspective of a participant trying to display the relationship while engaging in it. There is a strong emphasis on what we find ourselves doing and saying in certain contexts, Moreover, one of the unique features of the way in which these metaphors are presented is the dialogical format. The attempt is to get clear about what we already find ourselves doing in linguistic activity, and this attempt is carried on in dialogue with others, (the reader, hypothetical opponents, etc.) who are also participants.

This is not the place to speculate about historical and/or psychological factors that may have brought about this dramatic shift in Wittgenstein's way of approaching these questions which captivated his attention throughout his adult life. It can be noted, however, that the change of environment might have had something to do with it. His early work arose out of a somewhat rarified academic environment in which mathematics and logic played an important role. His later work, on the other hand, arose out of a fifteen year period away from philosophy, much of which was spent teaching school children in small mountain villages. This interaction with "the real world", where one is in direct contact with the process of learning and with the tasks of everyday life, may have shifted Wittgenstein's metaphorical anchorage.

As was the case in the Tractatus, nowhere in the Investigations does Wittgenstein offer any sort of justification for the root metaphors with which he constructs and presents his views. He does avoid the irony and embarrassment of a post-script which undercuts his whole enterprise, but he gives no indication from whence and why his metaphors have an authoritative "ring". A clue may well lie within his analysis of justification itself, but we shall postpone an exploration of this possibility until after the next chapter. For On Certainty deals with this very same issue and we will be in a better position from which to come at this important question after looking at it.

Once again it needs to be remarked that the literature on the role of metaphor in Wittgenstein's Philosophical Investigations is virtually non-existent. One searches in vain for some serious treatment of Wittgenstein's use of metaphor as a mode of philosophizing in such standard works as: A. Pitcher's The Philosophy of Wittgenstein (Englewood Cliffs: Prentice-Hall, 1964) and Wittgenstein: The Philosophical Investigations (Garden City: Doubleday, 1966), or K.T. Fann's Ludwig Wittgenstein: The Man and His Philosophy (New York: Dell, 1967), Mundle's A Critique of Linguistic Philosophy (Oxford: Oxford U.P., 1971), or G. Hallett's Wittgenstein's Definition of Meaning As Use (New York: Fordham Univ. Press, 1967). There are a few helpful remarks in A. Janik and S. Toulmin's Wittgenstein's Vienna (New York: Simon and Schuster, 1973) pp. 228 ff.

Chapter Six

--Metaphors in <u>On</u> <u>Certainty</u>--

During the last two years of his life Wittgenstein devoted a good deal of time to the
problems of certainty, and his notes from this
period have been collected and published in <u>On</u>
<u>Certainty</u>. Although the immediate context of
his concern is G.E. Moore's effort to justify
with certainty the belief in the existence of
the external world, the broader context is the
notion of certainty itself. In the course of
his explorations Wittgenstein once again makes
use of metaphorical expressions and tacks, many
of which are essentially the same as those introduced in the <u>Investigations</u>. There are, however,
certain moves unique to his final work which will
warrant special attention.

1. Practice and Function (<u>Praxis</u> <u>und</u> <u>Funktion</u>)

The main emphasis of the <u>Investigations</u>--
that meaning is a function of use--is also an
important theme in <u>On</u> <u>Certainty</u>. In fact, now
the notion is taken much more for granted, as an
obvious though mostly unspoken working premise.
Nevertheless there are passages where Wittgenstein makes the point quite explicitly. "A
meaning of a word is a kind of employment of it.
For it is what we learn when the word is incorporated into our language" (#61). Also: "Compare the meaning of a word with the 'function'
of an official. And 'different meanings' with
'different functions'" (#64). Thus in his view
meaning is a way of getting certain jobs done.

Here too, Wittgenstein stresses the cruciality of context in determining use. What constitutes the meaning of an utterance as mediated through one context may not figure into its meaning at all in yet another context. Once more he likens a particular way of speaking to a tool, since both derive their significance from their intended tasks as defined within a specific context.

> "Isn't the question 'Have these words
> a meaning?' similar to 'Is that a tool?'
> asked as one produces say, a hammer? I
> say 'Yes, it's a hammer'. But what if
> the thing that any of us would take for
> a hammer were somewhere else a missile,
> for example, or a conductor's baton?
> Now make the application yourself."
> (#351).

In the _Investigations_ Wittgenstein continually warned against trying to "distill" meaning of an utterance from an analysis of either the accumulation of the _prima facie_ meanings of its individual words or the activity of one's mind when making the utterance. The former move not only overlooks the fact that the meaning of the whole utterance may be quite distinct from the combined meanings of its parts (e.g. "When it rains it pours"), but it fails to take into account that the individual words acquire what appears to be their obvious meaning from (and _only_ from) their previous use within certain utterances. The latter move is irrelevant since two people may have (usually _do_ have) different things (images, associations, etc.) going on in their minds while nontheless communicating about a common meaning--and _vice versa_. Sameness of meaning is not dependent on sameness of image or process.

In _On Certainty_ Wittgenstein summarizes these points quite succinctly when he stresses the importance of practice (_praxis_):

> "There is always the danger of wanting to find an expression's meaning by contemplating the expression itself, and the frame of mind in which one uses it, instead of always thinking of the practice. That is why one repeats the expression to oneself so often, because it is as if one must see what one is looking for in the expression and in the feeling it gives one." (#601)

Another way to bring this functional quality of linguistic activity to the fore is by focusing on how and why certain utterances fail. Wittgenstein employs the metaphorical expression "misfire" (_fehlgeht_) when speaking of what happens when an utterance is misunderstood. The idea here is that since utterances are aimed at accomplishing certain tasks, their successful employment results in a "happy" connection while their unsuccessful employment results in a misunderstanding, a misfire. This way of speaking emphasizes the deed or activity dimension of speaking, as well as the possibility of corrections being made and understanding being finally achieved thereby.

Wittgenstein applies this way of speaking to the debate between idealists and realists over the reality of the external world. The only method of refuting those who would deny the reality of something may _not_ be to assert its reality, especially when it is a phenomenon as pervasive and primordial as belief in the existence of the external world. Wittgenstein suggests that the desire to defend such a

bedrock belief is understandable but out of
place, since the reality of the external world
shows itself in the activity of even the
idealist.

> "But is it an adequate answer to the
> scepticism of the idealist, or the
> assurances of the realist, to say that
> 'There are physical objects' is nonsense?
> For them after all it is not nonsense.
> It would, however, be an answer to say:
> this assertion, or its opposite is a mis-
> firing attempt to express what can't be
> expressed like that.  And that it does
> misfire can be shown; but that isn't
> the end of the matter.  We need to realize
> that what presents itself to us as the
> first expression of a difficulty, or of
> its solution, may as yet not be correct-
> ly expressed at all.  Just as one who has
> a just censure of a picture to make will
> often at first offer the censure where
> it does not belong, and an investigation
> is needed in order to find the right
> point of attack for the critic." (#37)


2.   The Language-Game of Doubt (Der Sprachspiel
                                 auf Zweifel)

     The whole idea of an utterance "misfiring"
is predicated on the notion of a language-game.
In order for a linguistic move to misfire there
must exist a conventional context within which
various moves are appropriate and others are
not.  Both the notion of convention and that of
activity are crucial here, for as was emphasized in the preceding chapter, the primary force
of the language-game metaphor is that of seeing
language as a way of doing things in addition
to simply uttering sentences.  Thus utterances

128

are seen as "moves" within an established but flexible pattern of social behavior, and those that are inappropriate to the language-game in question can be said to misfire.

Wittgenstein treats the whole notion of doubting as having viability only within the give-and-take of an established language-game.

> "The idealist's question would be something like: 'What right have I not to doubt the existence of my hands?' (And to that the answer can't be: I <u>know</u> that they exist.) But someone who asks such a question is overlooking the fact that a doubt about existence only works in a language-game. Hence, that we should first have to ask: what would such a doubt be like?, and don't understand this straight off." (#24)

Having located the phenomenon of doubting within the dynamic structure of a language-game Wittgenstein moves on to suggest some of the specific characteristics of the language-game of doubt. For one thing, "The game of doubting itself presupposes certainty" (#115). To put it differently, "Doesn't one need grounds for doubt?" (#122). Several times Wittgenstein offers the phrase "Everything speaks for it and nothing speaks against it" (#112-123) as a way of focusing his point here. For if indeed <u>everything</u> speaks for a belief or way of acting and <u>nothing</u> speaks against it, then both asserting it and denying it lie outside the language-game, they do not count as moves within it (#191, 192). And yet, of course, there remains a sense in which we want to say that the belief is justified, for it provides the general context within which more particular doubts and affirmations find their home.

> "That is to say, the _questions_ that we
> raise and our _doubts_ depend on the fact
> that some propositions are exempt from
> doubt, are as it were like hinges on
> which those turn." (#341)
> "That is to say, it belongs to the logic
> of our scientific investigations that
> certain things are _in deed_ not doubted."
> (#342) "But it isn't that the situation
> is like this: We just _can't_ investigate
> everything, and for that reason we are
> forced to rest content with assumption.
> If I want the door to turn, the hinges
> must stay put." (#343)
> "My _life_ consists in my being content to
> accept many things." (#344)

Another facet of the language-game of doubt
can be put in terms of logical priorities. While
to be certain in no way entails having doubted,
the act of doubting does necessitate having "a
place to stand" from which or within which one
can raise or focus the doubting. "Doubting and
non-doubting behavior. There is the first only
if there is the second" (#354). Psychologically
it works the same way. "The child learns by
believing the adult. Doubt comes _after_
belief" (#160).

A final characteristic of the doubting
language-game is that it takes place within
limits. As Wittgenstein maintained in the
_Investigations_ that precision is relative to
significance, so he maintains in _On Certainty_
that doubting is relative to effectiveness. As
one only needs as much precision as is necessary
for communication, so one only needs to doubt
when there are good reasons to do so. "What I
need to shew is that a doubt is not necessary

even when it is possible. That the possibility of the language-game doesn't depend on everything being doubted that can be doubted" (#392). Or, to paraphrase Kierkegaard, to try to teach a person to think by first teaching him to doubt is as silly as to try to teach a person to stand up straight by first teaching him to lie down in a heap.

One way of shifting the focus of the issue of the relation between doubt and certainty from the empirical level to the language-game level is to call attention to other dimensions or forces of utterances in which certainty is affirmed. Wittgenstein makes this move in #30 where he asserts that an affirmation of certainty is neither the basis nor the conclusion of an inferential process. Rather, its force is to communicate the degree to which one's judgment is to be relied upon. He employs the metaphor of "tone of voice" in making this point.

> "When someone has made sure of something, he says: 'Yes, the calculation is right', but he did not infer that from his condition of certainty. One does not infer how things are from one's own certainty.
>
> Certainty is as it were a tone of voice in which one declares how things are, but one does not infer from the tone of voice that one is justified." (#30)

To paraphrase J.L. Austin, when one claims that he knows (is certain) that such and such is the case he is not reporting on some superior act of cognition he has performed, but is rather affirming that he is in a position to know (has good reasons) and that others may relie upon his word.

131

## 3. Knowing As Doing (<u>Das</u> <u>Wissen</u> <u>Als</u> <u>Konnen</u>)

Circumscribing the language-game of doubting
in the foregoing fashion gives rise to yet another
major theme in <u>On</u> <u>Certainty</u> which is carried, at
least partially, by the force of metaphor. Like
those already dealt with in this chapter, the
present theme also has a clear counterpart in
the <u>Investigations</u>. In both works knowing (as
well as doubting) is seen as a form of human
behavior which is inextricably bound up with
certain ways of speaking. Together this behavior and way of speaking constitute a language-
game which governs such notions as knowing and
doubting. The particular characteristic of this
language-game which Wittgenstein finds epistemologically crucial is that of <u>activity</u>. At bottom, knowing is seen as a form of doing rather
than as a passive state.

Early on in <u>On</u> <u>Certainty</u> (#44-46) Wittgenstein introduces this theme when he distinguishes,
as he did in the <u>Investigations</u>, between "following a rule" in the sense of referring to a rule
when and as one proceeds in an activity and "following a rule" in the sense that one's activity
can be described as proceeding according to certain rules. He stresses that although the latter may often be the case, the former is <u>neces-</u>
<u>sary</u> neither to the original learning of the
activity nor to its being carried out. "We got
to know the nature of calculating  for example
by learning to calculate" (#45). And, "From a
child up I learnt to judge like this. <u>This</u> <u>is</u>
<u>judging</u>. This is how I learned to judge; <u>this</u>
I got to know <u>as</u> judgement" (#128,129). At the
outset one learns by imitation how to "react"
in certain ways in concrete contexts without
properly being said to "know" anything.

"Knowing only begins at a later level" (#538),
but it is from the outset anchored in "being _able
to do_ certain things" (#534).

The metaphorical force of this way of talking about knowing comes into play when Wittgenstein shifts to speaking of it as based in a
kind of decision to trust. In the midst of discussing the process of making various kinds of
judgments (about the earth, the dimensions or
even the advisability of a bridge, etc.) he asserts that all judgments must finally be based
in the process of judging itself, a process which
has no justification outside of itself. For,
"somewhere I must begin with an assumption or a
decision (_Entscheidung_)" (#146). A bit farther
on he asks:

> "How does someone judge which is his
> right and which his left hand? How do
> I know that my judgment will agree with
> someone else's? How do I know that this
> colour is blue? If I don't trust myself
> here, why should I trust anyone else's
> judgment? Is there a why? Must I not
> begin to trust somewhere? That is to
> say: somewhere I must begin with not-
> doubting; and that is not, so to speak,
> hasty but excusable: it is part of judg-
> ing." (#150)

Later on Wittgenstein approaches the issue
of the relation of evidence to questions of
truth and falsity from this same direction
(#197-200). Philosophers often make it sound
as though judgments about the truth value of a
proposition are made passively in the sense that
we simply see whether or not the evidence sup-
ports it, or whether or not it corresponds to
the facts. Wittgenstein makes it clear that
the logically prior question of what constitutes

evidential support, correspondence, and the like is itself a matter of judgment. Moreover, judgments at this level are based in decisions and actions rather than in passive "rubber-stamping" of whatever is dictated by the "facts" (#362). Apart from certain decisions and activities the concepts of support, correspondence, and even "fact" itself would have no meaning. "Knowledge (Wissen) is in the end based on acknowledgment (Anerkennung)" (#378).

Wittgenstein extends this way of looking at knowledge when he once again reminds us that justification comes to an end, "otherwise it wouldn't be justification". In this context he is especially concerned to make it clear that the end in which the justificatory process rests is not an irrational (or supra-rational), ungrounded leap of faith; nor is it a special act of cognitive insight.

> "Giving grounds, however, justifying the evidence, comes to an end;--but the end is not certain propositions' striking us immediately as true, i.e. it is not a kind of seeing on our part; it is our acting which lies at the bottom of the language-game." (#204)

Thus the process of justification is part of the human way of being in the world and it is grounded in the behavior and language-games which we have woven. To ask for a justification of the grounds of justification is to spin one's wheels. Not everything needs a justification outside of itself. The end of justification "is not an ungrounded presupposition: it is an ungrounded way of acting" (#110), which is to say, well established and fruitful ways of acting need no other grounds. A language-game "is not based on grounds. It is not reasonable (or unreasonable). It is there--like our life"(#599).

Another way to put this whole matter is in terms
of the distinction between saying and showing.
The grounds for our justificatory process, as well
as our other language-games, is our common social
activity, and while no justifications for these
need or can be articulated, they reveal themselves
tacitly in the course of our behavior.

"My life shews that I know or am certain
that there is a chair over there, or a
door, and so on.--I tell a friend e.g.
'Take that chair over there', 'Shut the
door', etc etc" (#7)
"But how can we shew someone that we know
truths, not only about sense-data but also
about things?  For after all it can't be
enough for someone to assure us that he
knows this.
Well, what must our starting point be if
we are to shew this?" (#426)  "We need
to shew that even if he never uses the
words 'K know...', his conduct exhibits
the thing we are concerned with." (#427)

It is perhaps debatable whether or not the
present theme is presented by means of metaphor
in On Certainty.  "Knowing" as a form of "doing"
may be taken quite literally.  I have treated it
as a metaphor primarily because the notion is so
radically different from the standard epistemological postures that it seems to stand in need
of an analogical explanation in order to gain a
hearing.  There can be no question, however
about the straight-forwardly metaphorical nature
of the moves to which we now turn our attention.

4.  The Human Form of Life (Der Menschen Lebens-
                                      form)

The foundation for all of the moves and

notions discussed thus far in this present chapter is what Wittgenstein has termed "the human form of life". This notion, while only used a half-a-dozen times or so in the _Investigations_ (and less than that in _On Certainty_) is nonetheless his most crucial epistemological contribution. Particular utterances find their meaning within the conventions and contexts of usage, and these in turn, along with justificatory processes, find their meaning within the activity of language-games as they are grounded in the patterns of behavior which comprise the human form of life. The unifying problem of _On Certainty_ is how best to speak about the confidence which arises from our active trust in this human form of life, how best to express the "reasonableness" of its finality.

It is when dealing with this problem that Wittgenstein turns most consistently and revealingly to the use of metaphor. The particular metaphors he employs are nearly as diverse as they are frequent. And yet even a cursory examination should suffice to bring out their overlapping similarities vis a vis the characterization of the ultimate resting place of all inquiries into the foundation of language and knowledge. In the following pages I shall note and discuss each metaphor in turn as it appears in the development of _On Certainty_. Some integrative remarks will be offered in the final section of the chapter.

a.  World-picture (_Weltbild_) #94-95.
     Here the Archemedian point from which, or the final criterion against which, one judges the truth and/or viability of any proposition or justificatory process is termed a "world-picture". Wittgenstein refers to it as an "inherited background" or "mythology" against or within which all other moves take on meaning

and are evaluated. Although the term "world-picture" suggests a parallel with the Tractatus, its conjunction with the term "mythology" makes it clear that Wittgenstein is using it quite differently here.

A bit farther on Wittgenstein introduces the notion of a system or structure within which meaning and verification take place but which can neither be described nor evaluated by these processes. Later still he says: "When we first begin to believe anything, what we believe is not a single proposition, it is a whole system of propositions...a system in which consequences and premises give one another mutual support...what stands fast does so, not because it is intrinsically obvious or convincing; it is rather held fast by what lies around it: (#141-144). (See also #211 where the term "scaffolding" is used.) The static quality of these metaphors is off-set by the introduction, in the last line of #105, of the metaphor of "the element (lebenselement) in which arguments have their life". This move suggests that human thought is dependent on the human way of being in the world in the same way that, say, fish are dependent on water.

b.  River-bed (Flussbett) #97-99)
Here the point is the contrast between empirical propositions and beliefs as a moving, flowing river and behavioral certainties as the unmoving channel within which the former flows. It is not as if the river-bed were unalterable, even though it controls the river, for the flow of the river can change the river-bed; but only slowly and never in a way that allows for a clear distinction between the two (#97). (See also #318-319).

137

"But if someone were to say 'So logic too is an empirical science' he would be wrong. Yet this is right: the same proposition may get treated at one time as something to test by experience, at another as a rule of testing." (#98)
"And the bank of that river consists partly of hard rock, subject to no alteration or only to an imperceptible one, partly of sand, which now in one place now in another gets washed away, or deposited." (#99)

c.  The Axis (Die Rotationsachse) #152

"I do not explicitly learn the propositions that stand fast for me. I can discover them subsequently like the axis around which a body rotates. This axis is not fixed in the sense that anything holds it fast, but the movement around it determines its immobility."
(#152)

There are two distinct major points to be noted in this metaphor. One pertains to the particular nature of the stability of our epistemological foundations. They are stable, not by virtue of being held in place (justified) by yet another system or entity (ad infinitum), but by virtue of the activities and developments which cluster around them. Their justification is embodied in their being. Secondly, our knowledge of these foundations, our certainty of or confidence in them, is neither learned nor articulated explicitly, but is discovered indirectly and relied upon tacitly in the give-and-take of everyday life.

138

d.  Rock Bottom/Foundation (<u>Der</u> <u>Boden/Grundlage</u>)

In two different passages Wittgenstein returns to the image he used several times in the
<u>Investigations</u>, namely that of "bedrock".  In
one of these passages (#246-254) he alternates
between 'foundation' (as the sub-structure of a
house) and 'rock bottom', while in the other
(#498) he employs the term 'bedrock' (<u>Fundamente</u>).
The basic force of the image is to locate that
point at which one can no longer make justificatory moves, not because of psychological reasons but because one has been brought up against
the grounds of justification itself.

"'Here I have arrived at a foundation of
all my beliefs.'  'This position I will
<u>hold</u>!'  But isn't that, precisely, only
because I am completely <u>convinced</u> of it?--
What is 'being completely convinced'
like?"  (#246)
"I have arrived at the rock bottom of my
convictions.  And one might almost say
that these foundation-walls are carried
by the whole house."  (#248)
"At the foundation of well-founded belief
lies belief that is not founded." (#253)
"Any 'reasonable' person behaves like
<u>this</u>." (#254)

There are two further points to be noted in
this the first passage.  One is that Wittgenstein
wishes to emphasize that the relation between
grounds and that which they support is in an
important sense reciprocal (#248).  One might
think here of the symbiotic relationship amongst
the stone blocks comprising a castle archway--
they both support and draw support from one
another.  Secondly, while "bedrock" beliefs are

139

"unfounded" (#253), this in no sense is to be construed as a weakness or as a point of departure for irrationalism. For those who participate in the human form of life ("reasonable" people) follow this pattern of behavior, they share this common activity (#254).

> "The queer thing is that even though I find it quite correct for someone to say 'Rubbish!' and so brush aside the attempt to confuse him with doubts at bedrock,--nevertheless, I hold it to be incorrect if he seeks to defend himself (using, e.g., the words 'I know')." (#498)

This second passage comes at these same questions from a different angle. When we are dealing with bedrock beliefs it not only makes no real sense to doubt them, it makes no sense to defend them by argumentation either. Bedrock must be allowed to show itself, for it is known tacitly (attended from). Therefore, all efforts to say (articulate) it misfire because they seek to make it explicit (attend to it). The appropriate response to those who seek to raise doubts about bedrock beliefs is to disallow their move ("Rubbish!"). Those who seek to rationally defend bedrock beliefs are worthy of more respect than this, but their efforts are misguided (#498,521).

e. Hinges (Die Angelin)

Yet another highly insightful metaphor used to characterize the cognitive structure of the human way of being in the world is that of "hinges". When discussing the possibility of doubt, Wittgenstein states that doubts depend on the fact that some propositions are "exempt from doubt, are as it were like hinges on which these turn" (#341). Later on (#655), while exploring the differences between bedrock certainties, (such as our own names) and mathematical propositions, he uses the hinge metaphor again to focus the nature and necessity of indisputable beliefs. And while at first he remarks that bedrock beliefs do not have the same incontestability as mathematical propositions, he concludes (#657) that in function the two types of certainties are similar.

f. Animal (<u>Animalisches</u>/<u>Tier</u>)

In the passage where he introduces the notion of "form of life" (#358), Wittgenstein goes on to characterize it as "beyond being justified or unjustified; as it were, as something animal" (#359). Elsewhere he says:

> "I want to regard man here as an animal; as a primitive being to which one grants instinct but not ratiocination. As a creature in a primitive state. Any logic good enough for a primitive means of communication needs no apology from us. Language did not emerge from some kind of ratiocination." (#475)

There are two important points which need to be mentioned here. First, the use of the term 'animal' in connection with 'forms of life' should dispel any suggestion that this latter notion connotes various types of postures within human existence, such as scientific, religious, Eastern,Western, Capitalist, Communist, etc. Rather, Wittgenstein would seem to have in mind distinctions among various forms of biological life, such as vegetable, animal and human. Next, it is important to remember that the distinguish-

141

ing feature here is language. Wittgenstein is
thinking of language as having an animal, instinctive basis rather than a rationalistic,
sophisticated one. A bit later (#499), he takes
the same position with regard to the "law of
induction". In fact, in one place he says:
"The squirrel does not infer by induction that
it is going to need stores next winter as well.
And no more do we need a law of induction to
justify our actions or our predictions" (#287).

g. Saddle/bucking (Sattel/bockten)

In #614-620 Wittgenstein considers the
question of when a person ought to give up on a
belief which has served as the hinge or axis of
his thought system. If, for example, everyone
suddenly began telling us that an old friend's
name really was not what we knew it to be, would
we acquiesce or hold on to our certain belief
in spite of the facts? Or, if nature suddenly
began to behave quite differently would we continue making inductive inferences in the manner
we do now? Wittgenstein concludes that if these
fixed points were removed "the foundation of
all judging would be taken away from me" (#614)
since such regularities are what make inferences
logically possible (#618).

This is not to say, however, that one cannot
imagine a person continuing to hold on to belief
in the face of every possible contrary fact; it
would not be "unthinkable that I should stay in
the saddle however much the facts bucked" (#616).
Indeed, it's possible that we could, if the
changes were not too drastic, adjust our form of
life to accommodate them, thereby adopting other
behavioral beliefs as our "saddle".

"Am I to say: even if an irregularity
in natural events did suddenly occur,

142

that wouldn't have to throw me out of
the saddle. I might make inferences then
just as before, but whether one would call
that "induction" is another question.
(#619)


5. Summary and Conclusion

There are many parallels between the Philosophical Investigations and On Certainty. Not
the least of them is the use of metaphors having
to do with human activity when treating such
notions as linguistic meaning and knowledge. In
this regard these two later books of Wittgenstein stand in contrast to the early Tractatus
which, as we have seen, is dominated by mathematical and spacial metaphors. They both make
strategic use of metaphors involving games, use,
behavior, judging, and deciding. The two later
works differ in some ways as well. Perhaps the
most obvious way is that whereas the Investigations is primarily concerned with linguistic
meaning in general, On Certainty deals mostly
with the language expressing epistemological
considerations in particular. The overall
philosophic posture of the two is essentially
the same.

There is one major development that takes
place in the transition from the Investigations
to On Certainty. In addition to the frequent
occurrance of human activity metaphors, there
is also the introduction, for the first time,
of a large number of metaphors having to do
with physical phenomena. We find metaphors involving river-beds, axis, bedrock, hinges, foundations, structure, animals, and bucking. Furthermore, while some of these metaphors focus
on human-made artifacts, the majority of them
center in the phenomena of nature. Thus the

root-metaphors of the three stages of Wittgenstein's work being considered undergo a marked transformation from (1) abstract, static space through (2) human activity and social behavior (3) to physical reality, especially that of the natural world.

To my mind this transformation is neither incidental nor accidental. It is not incidental because these metaphors clearly provide the backdrop against which, or better still, the ground out of which, the particular positions and conceptual moves of the works in question acquire their meaning and force. That this is so should be clear by now. The transformation is not accidental because it is part and parcel of the central enterprise in which Wittgenstein is engaged throughout his work. In all three of his major works he was looking for an adequate manner in which to characterize the nature of language, knowledge, and the world, and the relationship between them. In the Tractatus he carried a well established philosophical posture --that reality must be explained according to an intellectual pattern--to its logical end. The pure, abstract categories of logic were used to generate a static picture of language, knowledge, and the world. In the Investigations Wittgenstein shifted from the realm of the intellect to the realm of human social interaction as the basis of linguistic and cognitive activity in relation to the world. Finally, in On Certainty, he has begun to focus more on the "givens" of natural phenomena as the determinants of the human form of life.

There is no need to see these three stages of Wittgenstein's work as mutually exclusive. In the Investigations he does not deny any place of value to the metaphors of logical space, picturing, and the like. He simply shows how these metaphors are inadequate as total accounts of what meaning and knowledge are in relation to the world. In a word, he shows how these metaphors are based in and can only be justified in terms of the broader categories of human social behavior. In like manner, in On Certainty Wittgenstein does not set human social activity aside as a misleading metaphor, he rather seeks to show that such activity can only really exist and be understood by means of the patterns and character of metaphors of natural phenomena. In particular, he has moved to metaphors which locate human communication and understanding in the dialectic between human activity and the principles of nature. In a way Wittgenstein has come full circle; in the Tractatus he sought to explain the natural world on the basis of logical thought, in the Investigations he sought to explain logical thought on the basis of social activity, and in On Certainty he seeks to explain social activity on the basis of the natural world.

One further point about the naturalistic metaphors in On Certainty. By far the vast majority of them focus two inter-related emphases. The first is that of dynamism. The accent in almost every case is on the movement or interaction aspect of the metaphor. Hinges, rivers, axis, bucking saddles, and animal instincts all present a dynamic image as opposed to the static ones of the Tractatus. Secondly, in many cases there is a distinct vectorial character to these dynamic images. That is, the movement involved flows in one direction only, from the hinge, the axis, the river-bed to the door, the earch, and river, respectively.

The specific significance of this two-fold emphasis for the main concerns of On Certainty is, of course, epistemological. The dynamic quality of the metaphors carries with it the insight that knowledge is an active, relational

145

process rather than a passive, static state. Moreover, the vectorial quality of the metaphors stresses that we always know more than we can articulate and/or justify--and that this knowing is none-theless knowledge for being tacit and of bedrock character. In addition, we are justified in our knowing activity even though we can imagine the possibility of the hinges, the axis, or the river-bed of our thought being modified.

A final feature of On Certainty which bears on the notion of metaphor warrants brief discussion at this juncture. A more thorough exploration of this feature will comprise a good deal of Part Three of the present work. Throughout On Certainty we find discussions and topics introduced by such phrases as: "Supposing we met people who..." (#609-612), "Imagine that someone were to say..." (#332), "But imagine people who were..."(#338), "Suppose that I were the doctor...."(#461), etc. In addition we are frequently invited to consider cases of strange dialogue between teachers and students (#310ff) and doctors and patients (#461ff)--or to consider how we would react when confronted by hither-to unknown peoples (from Mars or the like) (#430, 338, 92).

There is a way in which this sort of "fantasy" can be thought of as a kind of metaphorical move, or at least as an analogical one, and although it is not without its counterpart in the Investigations it is much more frequent in On Certainty. The object seems to be to cast light on the structure of our present way of being in the world by juxtaposing it with other possible ways. Wittgenstein does not present these other possibilities in a complete fashion; indeed, he argues that this is impossible within our life form, since it would be tantamount to changing our present way of being in the world even to imagine a totally different one. Nevertheless, he does hope to place the hinges of our present form of life in some sort of relief by juxtaposing it with these fantasy or metaphorical situations.

There is very little literature on On Certainty itself, to say nothing of the role of metaphor therein. The general themes dealt with in this chapter receive some treatment in the following: (1) Barry Stroud, "Wittgenstein and Logical Necessity", Philosophical Review, vol. 74 (1965), pp. 504-518, (2) James Broyles "An Observation on Wittgenstein's Use of Fantasy", Metaphilosophy, vol. 5, No. 4., (3) Jerry H. Gill "On Reaching Bedrock", Metaphilosophy vol. 5, No. 4, and (4) Jerry H. Gill "Saying and Showing: Some Radical Themes in Wittgenstein's On Certainty", Religious Studies, vol. 10, pp. 279-290.

PART THREE


Chapter Seven

--Metaphor and Language--


It seems clear that Wittgenstein had no explicit theory of metaphor. It is just as clear,
however, that his writings contain an implicit
view of the nature and significance of metaphorical speech. In this chapter my aim is to surface this view by means of an examination of
Wittgenstein's employment of metaphor in his
three major works, together with a comparison
of these findings with the views discussed in
Part One.

### 1. A Summary of Wittgenstein's Use of Metaphor

In the <u>Tractatus</u> Wittgenstein sought to
ground linguistic meaning in the formal, abstract structure of language. Through an analysis of the logical relationship amongst words,
conceived of as an interlocking network of arbitrary symbols, he claimed to have explained both
the nature of language <u>per se</u> and the nature of
its relationship to the world. The root metaphor upon which this account of language and
reality was based was "logical space". In
essence this is a mathematical model, arising
most likely from Wittgenstein's early training
in engineering and his work with Russell in the
foundations of mathematics. The notion of

logical space carries with it certain correlative
notions which bear reviewing.

First, there are places and networks.  A
proposition is said to demarcate a place in logical space and this place is then thought of as
a "logical place".  Thus place is parallel to
point in geometry.  Moreover, all places in
logical space bear a relationship to one another,
a relationship which can be thought of as a network of lines joining points in space.  Once a
proposition has designated a place in logical
space, the whole network is in effect laid out
because space is both finite and determinant.

Second, the metaphor of logical space carries with it a visual perspective, and that in
two senses.  <u>Within</u> the view thereby espoused
the relation between reality and thought (as
well as language) is said to be one of "picturing".  The latter picture the former.  Sometimes
the imagery shifts to "mirroring", but the implications remain the same.  Also, <u>as</u> the view is
espoused the relation between it and the speaker
(Wittgenstein), together with the hearer, is a
visual one.  We are asked to <u>see</u> the relation
between language and reality in much the same
way as we would a vast but finite, perhaps two-
dimensional, space populated by points joined by
lines, in a grid-like fashion.  We are not placed within this space, but view it from outside.

Thirdly, it is clear that there is no action
or movement within logical space; it is static.
Points remain constant and the connections
among them do so as well.  This is not to say
that Wittgenstein maintained that language and
reality do not change and/or evolve.  It's just
that he was not interested in the dynamics of
and between language and reality.  He was,

150

rather, interested in their formal nature. In any given state, at any given instant, the relationships are what they are and from one instant to the next their logical character remains the same. In addition, once again we are on the outside of this world. There are no speakers nor hearers in logical space; there is no interaction, for Wittgenstein apparently thought that such considerations were unimportant to an understanding of language.

Finally, the logical space of the Tractatus is finite, it is bounded by limits. Now this raises a most interesting difficulty with respect to the place of metaphor in Wittgenstein's early work. It will be recalled that all the language (propositions) within logical space is specifically determined. Each utterance designates a single point, no more and no less. Thus there is no room for ambiguity and innovation, the very heart of metaphor. This same conclusion follows from the picture-theory of meaning. At the same time, however, the finite, limited character of logical space might suggest the possibility that metaphorical expression could find a home either on the other side of these limits or as the thin edge of the limits themselves. But, according to Wittgenstein, there is no significance outside of the limits. Even though he distinguished implicitly between nonsense and "the mystical" (the abortive utterances of ethics, aesthetics, and theology), there is no place in logical space for either.

Now the interesting difficulty arises when we consider the possibility of conceiving of metaphor as the thin edge of the limits themselves. This move is in fact suggested--perhaps necessitated--by the obvious metaphorical character of Wittgenstein's mode of presentation in the Tractatus. For he clearly is using a

151

mode of speech which itself has no home within logical space, and no linguistic significance can exist outside of it. From whence, then, derives the significance of Wittgenstein's overall view of significance itself? Wittgenstein's well-known way of treating this difficulty is to take back with his left hand what he had offered with his right hand. That is, he simply admitted that the logical space metaphor left no place for the presentation of it. However, he neither retracted his position nor his presentation of it.

It might be suggested that this difficulty could be avoided by "demetaphoricising" the view presented in the Tractatus, thereby eliminating the need to find a place for metaphor within the schema. This was the tack taken by Russell, Ayer, Carnap, et al in their various reductionistic maneuvers. None of these moves has proven successful, however, and Wittgenstein should be given credit for resisting this temptation. Not all utterances and terms, even in natural science, can be reduced to or transformed into observation statements or into statements which can be so reduced.

The crux of the difficulty, as well as the key to its solution, is forcefully focused in Wittgenstein's final, cryptic metaphor in the Tractatus, namely that of the ladder. He says that after understanding his presentation of logical space and its far-reaching correlates, which allow no room for the very metaphorical expressions upon which the view itself is based, after reaching such understanding we are to dispense with the presentation and its foundational metaphors. We are to "kick the ladder over after climbing up it". Clearly the main feature of the difficulty is that metaphorical expression is the necessary foundation for more explicit expression. The ladder that enables us to move from no expression to explicit expression is metaphoric expression. Thus it is not the sort of ladder which can be kicked over. For we are still and always standing on it!

Thus the key to the resolution of the difficulty is to acknowledge the bedrock character of metaphoric expression and to develop an account of language and its relation to reality which is in harmony with it in general, and which leaves room for it in particular. It is possible that it was this sort of consideration which troubled Wittgenstein and motivated him to rework his early theory. At any rate, he did return to philosophy after a fifteen year "retirement" because he felt a deep disquietude about his early views. Moreover, he did construct an essentially different view which in both form and content does provide a viable account of the place of metaphor in relation to language and reality. This view is powerfully expressed in the Philosophical Investigations.

In the Investigations Wittgenstein sought to ground meaning in human, social activity. Perhaps it is not important to speculate about the genesis of the metaphorical framework within which the later Wittgenstein came to operate. Nevertheless, it is not irrelevant to note that the sort of activities he was engaged in during his time away from philosophy (gardening, building a house, teaching in mountain villages, etc.) were drastically different from those which formed the background of the Tractatus. Nor is it difficult to see the connection between these activities and the main themes and metaphors of the Investigations. A brief review of these themes and metaphors will bring us to a clear understanding of the relation between his later view and the notion of metaphor in general.

153

To begin with, in the <u>Investigations</u> language is spoken of in <u>organic</u> metaphors. Speech is seen as a dynamic phenomenon which is alive in the sense that it is always changing; parts of it die off and new parts grow on. Thus language is alive both internally, in terms of its developing nature, and externally, in terms of its <u>functional</u> relation to the world. Language is not viewed as a static reflection of reality, but rather as an instrument by means of which reality is dealt with and altered. Moreover, it is "open-textured" in the sense that it is both flexible and evolving.

This organic motif is also carried out in two additional ways. Whereas the view of the <u>Tractatus</u> sought to be as abstract as possible, the approach in the <u>Investigations</u> is essentially <u>concrete</u>, i.e. it deals with specific utterances in particular contexts without trying to generalize about all linguistic expressions. Secondly, whereas the early Wittgenstein had viewed each individual proposition as inexorably linked with all others <u>via</u> a grand logical network, the later Wittgenstein saw individual utterances as having a corpuscular or <u>cellular</u> relationship with one another. Locating, adding, and/or eliminating one or more particular expressions from the whole does not necessarily locate or alter all the others.

Next, the organic and functional metaphors of the <u>Investigations</u> dove-tail smoothly with the overall emphasis on language as a human, social activity. The central notion of language-games is specifically employed to call attention to this important dimension of language, a dimension which had been systematically excluded from the <u>Tractatus</u>. The correlative metaphors of tools, handles, walking, chess playing, together with the stress placed on gesture,

154

intonation, and facial expression in determining meaning within context, all these serve to point up the kinesthetic quality of language. To put this slightly differently, there is a focus in the Investigations on the role of speakers as agents and as language as the medium of intentionality. Here again one sees (or better "feels") a marked contrast with the metaphors of the Tractatus which in no way involve interaction, whether between language and the world or between speakers and hearers.

In fact, this dynamic, interactive emphasis of the Investigations is carried over into its very form and structure. For its central stylistic characteristic is that of dialogical development, not in the heavy-handed fashion of Plato, but in the sense of honest wrestling with ideas and potential opponents, a kind of "thinking-out-loud". Here the metaphor of a labyrinth is especially important. The difference between a series of points located in logical space and the criss-crossing, overlapping maze-like character of a labyrinth is not simply that of order and precision versus nonuniformity and ambiguity. Equally as important is the fact that one is on the outside looking in with respect to the former, while one is inside the latter. This represents a crucial change in standpoint from the early work of Wittgenstein to the later. For the external position gives one the delusion of objectivity, that total order and precision are possible, while the internal standpoint forces one to see that such goals are both unattainable and unnecessary.

One final aspect of this organic, functional view needs to be mentioned, and that is its social dimension. In the Investigations language is portrayed as part of the social, public fabric of human existence, not as existing independently of life, nor as the result of

155

a single, LaPlace-like thinker's dream.  Language
is a <u>community</u> enterprise, arising out of and
finding its meaning in the social matrix of
inter-personal and institutional interaction.
Here, too, the placement of language <u>in</u> the
world, and of speakers within language, completely avoids the kind of solipsistic and skeptical
muddles generated by the approach of the <u>Trac-
tatus</u>.  It does so by choosing a different starting point and arguing that the traditional philosophical muddles are abstractions which themselves stand in need of justification in terms
of concrete human speech, and not vice versa.

What, then, of metaphor?  As has been said,
the organic, functional approach to language which
characterizes the <u>Investigations</u> carries with it
the correlative notion that language possesses
and "open-textured" quality.  There are at least
two aspects of this quality which bear directly
on the question of the nature of metaphorical
expression.  First off, conceived of in this way
language cannot be said to have a particular
unified, underlying structure which accounts
for the overall phenomenon of meaning.  In the
<u>Tractatus</u> Wittgenstein had reduced all "official"
meaning to a function of either empirical or
logical statements, and was then obliged to ban
a large percentage of human language (namely
ethics, aesthetics, and theology) from the realm
of the meaningful.  He maintained that all meaningful language has essentially the same structure and/or purpose.  The insights of the <u>Inves-
tigations</u> render this early approach quite inadequate, since it now appears that not all cases
of meaningfulness have a common underlying character.  Each particular utterance obtains its
meaning from the context and language-game which
surrounds it, since these determine the purpose
or function of the utterance.  Thus meaning is
a function of use.

156

This aspect of the open-textured quality of language eliminates the possibility and the necessity of reducing all meaningful discourse to a single kind, thus opening the way for metaphoric meaning. Not only has this type of reduction not been carried out, it is in principle impossible according to Wittgenstein because the sort of precision involved must necessarily be based on processes and meanings which are themselves imprecise. Children do not begin, after all, with clear and distinct definitions of the terms they employ when acquiring language. Precision comes later, as needed. Thus it is a pragmatic and contextual notion, not a prerequisite. Nor do we, as adult users of language, fall back on precise definitions in order to give our utterances meaning. Nor <u>can</u> we, in most cases, if pressed. Rather, we begin with vagueness and ambiguity, and move <u>toward</u> precision as it seems helpful.

> "To repeat, we can draw a boundary-- for a special purpose. Does it take that to make the concept usable? Not at all! (Except for that special purpose.) No more than it took the definition: 1 pace= 75 cm. to make the measure of length 'one pace' usable. And if you want to say 'But still, before that it wasn't an exact measure', then I reply: very well, it was an inexact one--though still you owe me a definition of exactness.(#69)
> "But if the concept 'game' is uncircumscribed like that, you don't really know what you mean by a 'game'. When I give you the description: 'The ground was quite covered with plants'--do you want to say I don't know what I am talking about until I can give a definition of a plant?" (#70)

The second aspect of the open-texture of language, which is relevant to a consideration of metaphor, is that pertaining to the evolution of language. As Wittgenstein notes, new expressions and language-games are continually being incorporated into language while others are continually being left behind.

Thus innovation and obsolescence are important features of any natural language. One of the primary bearers of innovation is metaphor, for it often takes the form of combining two fairly well-established meanings to produce a fresh one. It is this feature of innovation which goes unaccounted for in the _Tractatus_, even though it itself is clearly dependent upon it. Here again we see that the view of language put forth in the _Investigations_ is congenial to the notion of metaphoric meaning by reason of its stress on the flexibility and functionality of linguistic phenomena.

Even though some innovations are a result of scientific discoveries and/or stipulations, it remains the case that language functions quite well, though "incomplete", _and_ that innovations of the "precising" kind are logically parasitic on metaphoric ones, since we must stand somewhere as we do the precising.

"Do not be troubled by the fact that languages (2) and (8) consist only of orders. If you want to say that this shews them to be incomplete, ask yourself whether our language is complete; --whether it was so before the symbolism of chemistry and the notation of the infinitesimal calculus were incorporated in it; for these are, so to speak, suburbs of our language. (And how many houses or streets does it take before a town begins to be a town?) Our language can be seen as an ancient city; a maze of little streets and squares, of old and new houses, and of houses with additions from various periods; and this surrounded by a multitude of new boroughs with straight regular streets and uniform houses." (#18)

Given the foregoing considerations, it is hardly surprising to find that nowhere in the Investigations does Wittgenstein show the slightest tendency toward being embarrassed about his frequent, indeed pivotal, use of metaphor. There is an essential harmony between content and form in the Investigations which stands in complete contrast to the Tractatus. In form the two books are similar in the sense that they both rely heavily upon metaphorical expression and understanding. They differ in that the content of the one leaves no room for such expressions and understandings, while that of the other not only makes room for them, but places them at the heart of language.

"The more narrowly we examine actual language, the sharper becomes the conflict between it and our requirement. (For the crystal-line purity of logic was, of course, not a result of investigation: it was a requirement.) The conflict becomes intolerable; the requirement is now in danger of becoming empty.--We have got onto slippery ice where there is no friction and so in a certain sense the conditions are ideal, but also, just because of that, we are unable to walk. We want to walk: so we need friction. Back to the rough ground!" (#107)

From a linguistic point of view On Certainty is quite similar to the Investigations. Many of the same metaphors and themes are presented by way of developing an understanding of language which is at once viable and fruitful. The emphasis on language as an activity within roughly defined language-games is repeated, as is the characterization of meaning as a function of use in context. In addition, some fresh metaphors are introduced, ones which pertain more to physical or natural reality than to human, social reality. Hinges, foundations, animals, riverbeds, bedrock, and axis all figure in. Here again it is important to note that the view of language employed is of a piece with this use of metaphor.

The major thrust of On Certainty is, however, epistemological rather than linguistic. In many ways it appears as a natural sequel to the Investigations, since it deals with the question of the justification of language-games, especially those surrounding certain kinds of knowledge claims. This is a subject which Wittgenstein raised in the Investigations, but left largely unexplored. This exploration is carried on in On Certainty within the broad perspective on language introduced in the Investigations. Nevertheless, its focus on epistemological issues renders a more detailed consideration of its bearing on metaphor more appropriate in the third section of the present chapter.

## 2. A Comparison With Interactionists

With the foregoing summary before us, we can turn now to a specific comparison of the view of metaphor inherent in Wittgenstein's work with the views sketched out in Chapters One and

160

Two.  The work of the early Wittgenstein bears
interesting relationships to the views of metaphor espoused by Tillich and Edwards.  On the one
hand, Tillich's view is based on a simple dichotomy between signs and symbols, the former func-
tioning as names of objects, qualities, and aspects of perceptual reality and the latter func-
tioning as metaphorical mediators of non-percep-
tual reality.  Signs yield representational meaning since they <u>point</u> <u>to</u> their referent, while
symbols yield existential meaning since they
<u>participate</u> <u>in</u> the reality to which they refer.
Unfortunately Tillich does not provide a thorough
enough exploration of this dichotomy to render it
very helpful in coming to grips with the notion
of metaphor.  Moreover, the more or less exclusively theological application of the distinction
is problematic, especially since Tillich claims
that in the statement "God is Being itself" the
term 'God' functions in a non-symbolic, referential fashion.  Such a move leads to difficulties
which are all too familiar.

On the other hand, Edwards' view of metaphor is based on a straight-forward reducibility
criterion, according to which any metaphor which
cannot be <u>translated</u> into a literal, observational statement (the latter serving as a"substitution" for the former) is said to be without
cognitive meaning.  The difficulties with this
approach were discussed in Chapter One.  In
addition to being at best a stipulation or proposal, rather than an empirical conclusion, this
approach entails that "literal" or precise language is logically prior to metaphorical or ambiguous and vague language.  That this is a long
way from being established, indeed that it is
diametrically opposed to what is the case, was
adumbrated in the foregoing discussion of the
insights of Wittgenstein's <u>Investigations</u>.
Moreover, it is a point to which we shall return.

161

Now, the view of metaphor inherent in the
Tractatus is something of a mixture of the views
of Tillich and Edwards. "Officially" Wittgenstein adheres to the reducibility theory, with
all meaningful utterances being viewed as truth
functions of elementary propositions which mirror
atomic facts. Thus utterances which seek to do
"more" than this, including metaphorical ones,
actually do "less". "What can be said at all
can be said clearly. Whereof we cannot speak,
we must remain silent." At the same time, however, "unofficially" Wittgenstein admitted that
this view itself is incapable of being articulated within the confines which it sets. Some
form of expression beyond representational signification must be allowed for, if only to make
possible the criteria-establishing function of
philosophy. In addition, Wittgenstein's self-
acknowledge "nonsensical" remarks about God,
death, life, the soul, and values ("the mystical") seem to fall back on some form of symbolic expression, à la Tillich. The tension between the official and unofficial views of the
Tractatus, both integral to it, is left unsolved.

More importantly it must be borne in mind
that the primary mode in which Wittgenstein pro-
pounds his early view is the metaphorical mode.
Thus it is not simply a matter of his view not
leaving room for talk about certain aspects of
experience (including the view itself), but it
is a matter of leaving no room for the very mode
of speech within which the view itself is expressed. According to standard logical empiricist theory this difficulty can be resolved by
expressing the same view (propositions!) in non-
metaphorical language. This move, however, begs
the question, for that is the very issue at
stake and the tension between the official and
unofficial views of the Tractatus makes this
abundantly clear. Thus the need for a more

162

sophisticated and fruitful understanding of
language in general and metaphor in particular
is brought into focus.

The view embodied in Wittgenstein's use of
metaphor, as well as in his explicit posture toward language, in both the Investigations and
On Certainty is essentially different from the
views discussed directly above, including that of
the Tractatus. Moreover it goes a long way toward providing the framework for a sufficiently
rich and fruitful understanding of language and
metaphor to meet the need focused by the enig-
matic character of the Tractatus. The foundation for such an understanding is provided in
On Certainty, especially as it relates to the
insights of Michael Polanyi. This consideration
will be taken up in the next chapter.

Many of the same results are to be gathered
from a comparison of Wittgenstein's use of metaphor with the views of Langer and Turbayne as
arose from the foregoing comparison with Tillich
and Edwards. As was pointed out in Chapter One,
Langer's efforts to counter the self-imposed
poverty of logical empiricism, or linguistic re-
ductionism, by constructing a parallelism between discursive thought and speech on the one
hand and presentational expression on the other
have their basis in the very same dualism which
underlies Wittgenstein's position in the Tractatus. Both thinkers stress the distinction between saying and showing, with Wittgenstein
identifying the latter with linguistic silence
and Langer connecting it with artistic expression.
Langer's view is surely the richer of the two,
but both ultimately founded on the question of
the cognitivity of metaphoric thought and expression.

163

The ironic thing is that both Langer and the
Wittgenstein of the _Tractatus_ have within their
work the seeds for a more comprehensive and holistic understanding of language, one which grants
a primary role to the metaphoric mode. As was
mentioned in Chapter One, Langer herself affirms
the primoridal, all-pervasive character of _poetic_
and _metaphoric_ speech without sensing the destruc-
tive significance of this insight for her own
highly delineated dualism. In like manner, she
stresses the _presentational_ thrust of artistic
expression while failing to acknowledge this same
dynamic within linguistic expression. The two
sides of her dualism can be, indeed should be,
united by means of the metaphoric basis of all
expression. As we have seen in Chapter Four,
Wittgenstein's _use_ of the metaphoric mode in the
_Tractatus_ runs counter to, and finally undercuts,
the central claims of this work concerning what
can and cannot be said. This tension is overcome in the _Investigations_ wherein the view of
language as open-textured not only makes room
for the cognitivity of metaphor but demands it.
Here there is harmony between the content and
the metaphorical mode of presentation.

Roughly the same situation obtains in relation to the comparison between Wittgenstein and
Turbayne. Like the early Wittgenstein, Turbayne
wants to claim _both_ that metaphor is _only_ metaphor (and is therefore somehow inferior) _and_
that we can never free ourselves from metaphor
(in the _Tractatus_ this is not said but shows
itself). Turbayne wants to kick his ladder over
and stand on it at the same time, but whereas
Wittgenstein implicitly acknowledges the obvious inconsistency of this move, Turbayne seems
unaware of it. Here, too, the understanding of
language developed in the _Investigations_ over-
comes this inconsistency by removing the assumption implicit within Turbayne's approach that

164

metaphoric or non-precise language is essentially
inferior. Thus the later Wittgenstein can express his insights metaphorically without embarrassment, whereas Turbayne must engage in the
slight-of-hand of "exposing" metaphor by means
of a metaphor of his own.

The view of metaphor inherent in Wittgenstein's later work is best understood in relation to those presented by Wheelwright and Black.
To begin with, there is a harmony between what
Wittgenstein says about the character of language
and his use of language. That is to say, one of
his overall themes is that significant precision
is sufficient for meaningfulness; that all moves
toward increased precision must arise out of and
depend upon a context the elements of which are
themselves remain "imprecisely" defined but nonetheless meaningful. Thus a reliance upon terms
and concepts which are not reducible to truth
functions of observational statements is not an
embarrassment to the Wittgenstein of the Investigations. More specifically, the positive employment of metaphorical expressions as the vehicle of a philosophical position on the nature of
language turns out to be not only admissable but
necessary. The epistemological dimension of
this point will be taken up shortly.

An examination of the specific metaphors
of the Investigations and On Certainty reveals
their "interactionary" character. The central
metaphor of language-games is especially fruitful in this regard. The combining of the notion
of languages with that of games both depends upon
what Wheelwright calls a "diaphoric" element and
creates what he terms an "epiphoric" element.
The established differences between the two
notions generates an energy which is at once
exploded and synthesized in their combination

165

and interaction. We do, in fact, begin to get
fresh ideas about what language is when we consider its similarities with games: both are
activities, both are social, functional, in some
sense rule governed, and their justifications
lies outside of them. At the same time we are
given fresh ideas about games when they are jux-
taposed with language: games can be thought of
as systems of communication in which each move
signifies something, and they may be viewed as
ways of getting certain things accomplished.
This "two-directional" meaning exemplifies
Black's interaction theory of metaphor, and is
capable of being extended to many of the other
basic metaphors in Wittgenstein's later writings.

Such considerations bring up what might be
termed the "revelatory" character of metaphor,
about which both Black and Wheelwright speak.
Here too there seems to be a parallel between
their insights and what Wittgenstein both says
and does with metaphor. His general placing
of precision language as logically ancillary to
multi-significant and rough-edged language implies that the latter is closer and more useful
to that level of experience wherein insights are
generated. Thus when one wishes to express a
quality or relationship freshly perceived or conceived, the first move is made, of necessity, in
a form which hopefully alters the established
patterns of speech enough to reveal the insight
but not so much as to be incomprehensible. Furthermore, even though some of these original
locutions may, and indeed for certain purposes
should, be rendered into more precise terminology,
it remains the case that not all of them can be
so rendered. For in the final analysis precision
is based on making stipulations, and stipulations
must be expressed in pre-stipulative or imprecise
language.

Finally, it should be noted that Wittgenstein's own employment of metaphor clearly and forcefully bears out the foregoing observations. For in his later work he relied, at the fundamental level, on metaphor to convey his own fresh insights. He unapologetically introduces his key ideas and carries on his dialogical enterprise by means of metaphoric expressions. Furthermore, to the extent that his early work conveys the power and clarity of a fresh insight, to that extent it too exhibits the primordial character of metaphor, in spite of the fact that his early view undercut its own mode of presentation. The genius and influence of Wittgenstein's later work, whether or not one agrees with him on specific philosophical issues, lies in its revelatory quality, and that quality is directly dependent on the far-reaching force of his metaphors. In the terminology of Black, he sought to provide a fresh "focus" for the notions of meaning and philosophy by inviting us to experience them through the "framework" of such common phenomena as games, tools, and getting about.

The interactionist thrust of Wittgenstein's later work runs parallel to the insights of Beardsley and Percy as well as to those of Black and Wheelwright. Perhaps the main point of connection between the views of Beardsley and Wittgenstein lies in their mutual emphasis on the importance of context to meaning. Beardsley's stress on what a metaphor "says" and what it "suggests", as well as his recent concern with the relation between speaker and hearer vis a vis "credence-properties", is in harmony with Wittgenstein's emphasis on use and interaction. Moreover, there is agreement between them concerning the "incomplete" and flexible nature of language; both affirm the impossibility and non-necessity of formalizing the

167

patterns of meaning in a set of rules. Here, again, we see that Wittgenstein's <u>use</u> of metaphor embodies a view of metaphor as both primordial and cognitive. Beardsley's willingness to call a given metaphor "true" (or "apt") is not unlike Wittgenstein's concern to ground meaning and language-games in the human form of life. But more of this in the next chapter.

Like Walker Percy, Wittgenstein is concerned to forge a position between, or which transcends, the standard options of behaviorism and dualistic rationalism (à la Chomsky). Both Percy and Wittgenstein stress the <u>relational</u> and/or "public" character of meaning as mediated through sound and gesture without being reducible to them. Furthermore, both Percy and Wittgenstein develop their thought along lines which parallel the insights made available by continental phenomenologists. These parallels will be spelled out better in connection with the views of Gadamer, Merleau-Ponty, and Ricoeur.

Wittgenstein and Percy agree, in addition, that language, far from being optional and/or arbitrary, constitutes a <u>sine qua non</u> of being human. It is through participating in speech within a linguistic community that we become human. At the bedrock level there exists a confluence of speech and reality whereby they constitute each other. Thus language, especially in its primordial metaphoric mode, provides the fabric within which we come to know the world. Percy speaks of "coupling" and "pairing" reality and language by means of the act of speaking, while Wittgenstein stresses language-games and certain proto-activities as providing the hinges for our interaction with the world. Both thinkers thereby affirm the cognitive character of such primoridal behavior, since it is out of this that notions of the 'real' and the 'true' arise.

## 3. A Comparison With Constitutivist Views

The above themes carry us over into a consideration of the relation between Wittgenstein's use of metaphor and the views presented in Chapter Three. By and large such thinkers as Nelson Goodman, Paul Ricoeur, Owen Barfield, and phenomenologists like Gadamer and Merleau-Ponty, have much in common with the interactionists discussed in the previous section. What distinguishes these thinkers from the interactionists is their explicit committment to a view of metaphor as constitutive of reality in addition to being revelatory thereof. It is now time to ask about the relation of Wittgenstein's use and view of metaphor to this way of viewing the metaphoric mode. The focus will be on the later work of Wittgenstein, since it already has been established that the early work, albeit inconsistently, leaves no room for such a point of view.

In my opinion there is a strong constitutivist strain in Wittgenstein's work, both in its form and in its content. With respect to content, there is the unmistakable emphasis on the confluence of what is said - meaning, truth, and reality - and the way it is said - use, context, and language games - at the bedrock (or "form of life") level. Logic, behavior, and speech are inextricably woven together at the most fundamental level, so that it makes no sense to talk about standing apart from any of them, or about justifying one in terms of the other. The following quotations, the first from the Investigations and the second from On Certainty, serve to pin-point this constitutive emphasis in Wittgenstein's later thought.

"So you are saying that human agreement
decides what is true and what is false?"
--It is what human beings _say_ that is true
and false: and they agree in the _language_
they use. That is not agreement in opinions but in form of life.
If language is to be a means of communication there must be agreement not only in
definitions but also (queer as this may
sound) in judgments. This seems to abolish
logic, but does not do so.--It is one
thing to describe methods of measurement,
and another to obtain and state results
of measurement. But what we call "measuring" is partly determined by a certain
constancy in results of measurement.
(#241-242)

Giving grounds, however, justifying the
evidence, comes to an end;--but the end
is not certain propositions' striking us
immediately as true, i.e. it is not a
kind of _seeing_ on our part; it is our
_acting_, which lies at the bottom of the
language-game. (#204)

Although there are many similarities between
the constitutive thrust of Wittgenstein's later
thought and that of Nelson Goodman, there is at
least one major difference as well. This difference revolves around the question of whether
or not our ways of speaking, or to use Goodman's
phrase, our ways of "world-making", are entirely
relative. I shall deal more pointedly with the
epistemological aspect of this question in the
next chapter (and again briefly in the final
chapter, in connection with the thought of Thomas Kuhn). At this juncture it is sufficient to
point out that the difference between Goodman
and Wittgenstein revolves around the manner in

which they present their constitutivist positions.

Even though Goodman affirms that the many different worlds we make through our linguistic endeavors are "actual" (and not mythological) worlds, he nonetheless chooses to express this affirmation in relatively non-metaphoric speech. Wittgenstein, on the other hand, couches his constitutivism in the metaphoric mode itself. Goodman's approach still creates the impression that he is giving an "objective" account of the fact that an objective account is impossible. Wittgenstein's approach, however, uses metaphors to express the logical priority of the metaphoric mode. Moreover, Wittgenstein's way of weaving speech, behavior, and logic together in the notion of bedrock separates his view from the relativism of Goodman's view. The former thinks there is a final justification for the way we speak, namely our "form of life" itself, while the latter denies such a bedrock. We shall return to this issue in the next chapter.

Wittgenstein's understanding of the metaphoric mode seems much closer to that of Paul Ricoeur. Both seek to go beyond the relativism of Goodman's position without becoming entangled in some form of "objective" metaphysics. Wittgenstein seeks to ground our primordial speech in our interactive behavior in relation to physical and social reality, while Ricoeur speaks of the dual thrust of the basic act of prediction, the pivotal "is" and "is not" of all affirmation. Interestingly enough, Ricoeur continues to speak in non-metaphoric mode when expressing his insights, while Wittgenstein consistently remains within the metaphoric mode when urging his point of view. The latter procedure would seem more consistent with the overall point being made about the primacy of metaphor.

171

Perhaps the point of closest agreement between Ricoeur and Wittgenstein is to be found in the appropriateness of the symbiotic model to both their postures. For both thinkers language and reality seem to be viewed as _mutually_ constitutive of one another. Like the poles of a magnetic field, language and the world are only definable and knowable in relation to each other; indeed, they only _exist_ in relation to each other. Moreover, both Ricoeur and Wittgenstein stress the cruciality of human participation in bringing these two poles into relationship. At the primordial level both thinkers affirm the primacy of the metaphoric mode to this participatory process. However, both agree, against Goodman, that the logical priority of metaphor does not entail an ontological relativism, that there is a way of crowding between or transcending the objectivist-subjectivist dichotomy. This way is through metaphoric speech and understanding. Ricoeur affirms the practice thereof and Wittgenstein embodies the affirmation in his practice.

The connections between Wittgenstein's later use and implied theory of metaphor on the one hand and the points of view of the remaining thinkers presented in Chapter Three on the other hand should be fairly obvious. Although there are significant differences as well, all of these thinkers share with Wittgenstein the conviction that at the deepest level metaphoric speech is a kind of "protophenomenon" whereby the world takes on its reality in relation to human existence. There are also tends to be, though with some more than others, a concern to place or ground language in general and metaphoric speech in particular within the broader spectrum of human _activity_. Speech is a form of behavior, and behavior is a form of speech-- and the metaphoric mode would seem to be the point of intersection between the two.

Gadamer stresses game playing, Merleau-Ponty emphasizes the role of the body, while Barfield insists on the connection between meaning and sound (onomatopoeia). One might call this a "somatic syndrome" because of the overlapping focus on the role of embodied activity in language and understanding. Wittgenstein, too, exhibits this somatic syndrome in his later writings when he grounds meaning and knowledge in physical and social behavior, not arbitrarily but constitutively. The epistemological implications of this grounding will be the topic of the next chapter.

One helpful way of summarizing Wittgenstein's implicit view of metaphor might be in terms of the notion of metonymy. For not only does he use metaphor in such a way as to imply that he views it as logically primitive and constitutive in relation to experienced reality, but his own use and examples of metaphor serve as paradigmatic samples or iconic symbols of this relationship. The part, in this case Wittgenstein's own metaphoric expressions, stands for the whole, namely the nature of the metaphoric mode as such. This way of putting the matter suggests that Wittgenstein viewed philosophical explorations themselves as metaphoric in character, that his way of doing philosophy was itself an example of and invitation to participate in the making of metaphors. This suggestion will be pursued in the final chapter.

Chapter Eight

--Metaphor and Cognition--


The crucial issue emerging from the foregoing discussion, and indeed from this study as
a whole, pertains to the nature of the relationship between metaphor and cognitivity. More
pointedly, the question arises concerning the
connection between the constitutive character
of metaphoric speech, vis a vis experienced
reality, and the epistemological status of bedrock ways of thinking and/or behaving. This
connection is focused in Wittgenstein's later
writings, especially On Certainty, at the point
where his own use of metaphor and his notion of
"form of life" intersect. For at the most fundamental level, Wittgenstein's own investigations
rest on certain pivotal metaphors about the relation between knowledge and the world, and quite
obviously are intended to provide a truthful
account of this relation.

The purpose of this chapter is to offer an
examination of the epistemological posture entailed by Wittgenstein's metaphorical treatment
of knowledge in On Certainty. I shall urge that
a rubric which provides a most helpful way of
understanding Wittgenstein's position is that of
tacit knowing, as developed by Michael Polanyi.
My conclusion will be that metaphoric expression
is the most appropriate, if not the only, mode
for communicating the bedrock truths about the
world and our way of being in it, because such
truths can only be known tacitly. The more
fundamental the knowledge, the less direct can

175

be its expression, since the expression itself embodies, and thus relies upon, the knowledge in question. Thus the primordial character of the metaphoric mode. Both the content and the form of On Certainty, as well as of the Investigations, reveal that Wittgenstein knew this.

### 1. Main Themes in On Certainty

On the surface level, On Certainty is concerned with the problem of the existence of the external world. More specifically, it is a puzzlement over how to deal with G.E. Moore's "Proof of an External World". There are a number of passages wherein Wittgenstein worries over some of the particulars of Moore's 'proof' of holding up his two hands and calling attention to them as external objects. He also worries over what it can mean to list various things that one knows-- and that everyone knows-- about the physical world, as Moore does in his "A Defense of Common Sense". The most concise statement of Wittgenstein's stance with regard to Moore is, 'Moore's mistake lies in this-- countering the assertion that one cannot know (some things about the external world), by saying "I do know it"' (#521).

This remark engages other themes more central than that of the existence of the external world. One such theme is whether or not it is proper to speak of those maintaining a scepticism about the external world as 'mistaken'. In addition to suggesting that to speak in such a way would be like saying that we have all been mistaken in all or our calculations, (#55) Wittgenstein declares:

'In certain circumstances a man cannot make a mistake. ("Can is here used logically, and the proposition does

176

not mean that a man cannot say anything false in those circumstances.) If Moore were to pronounce the opposite of those propositions which he declares certain, we should not just share his opinion: we should regard him as demented.' (#155)

Another theme engaged by the previous remark Moore's mistake is that of the logic of the locution, 'I know...'. The first thing that strikes one about Wittgenstein's treatment of this theme is the similarity it bears to that of Austin's in his essay on "Other Minds". The performative or illocution-way thrust ('I know' is like 'I promise') of knowledge claims stressed by Austin is precisely that focused on by Wittgenstein. Thus, one is entitled to use the term 'know' without implying that one cannot be wrong. He is, however, _giving_ _his_ _word_ (#176) that he has _good_ _reason_ to make his assertion. (#18)

It would be wrong to say that I can only say 'I know that there is a chair there' when there is a chair there. Of course it isn't true unless there is, but I have a right to say this if I am _sure_ there is a chair there, even if I am _wrong_. (#549)

One more theme comprising the cluster around the central issue needs to be unpacked before moving on. The troubles over (1) saying 'I know...; with respect to positive assertions about the existence of the external world, (2) saying that denials of the existence of the external world are 'mistaken', and (3) knowing being confused with the impossibility of being wrong, all lead Wittgenstein to raise serious questions about the viability of so-called 'doubts' about such bedrock considerations as the existence of the external world. He argues that there must be grounds for doubting, just

177

as there must be grounds for believing; that doubting must take place <u>within</u> a language-game, and thus cannot be engaged in willy-nilly; and that doubt is parasitic on belief, since the latter is both psychologically and logically prior. These conclusions are forcefully and graphically summarized in the following passage where Wittgenstein suggests that a teacher would rightfully become impatient with a student who raised questions about <u>esse ist percipi</u>.

> 'That is to say, the teacher will feel that this is not really a legitimate question at all.
> And it would be just the same if the pupil cast doubt on the uniformity of nature, that is to say on the justification of inductive arguments.--The teacher would feel that this was only holding them up, that this way the pupil would only get stuck and make no progress.--And he would be right. It would be as if someone were looking for some object in a room; he opens a drawer and doesn't see it there; then he closes it again, waits, and opens it once more to see if perhaps it isn't there now, and keeps on like that. He has not learned to look for things. And in the same way this pupil has not learned how to ask questions. He has not learned <u>the</u> game that we are trying to teach him. (#315)

In connection with several passages dealing with the nature of doubt, Wittgenstein uses the phrase 'Everything speaks for it and nothing against it' to refer to a belief that somehow seems beyond doubt. Here again he puzzles over how to speak of the epistemological status of these beliefs--they cannot be doubted, since

178

there are no grounds for doubting them; yet it seems odd to call them 'certain' in the usual sense, because any attempt to justify them presupposes them.

> 'Well, if everything speaks for an hypothesis and nothing against it--is it then certainly true? One may designate it as such.--But does it certainly agree with reality, with the facts?-- With this question you are already going round in a circle.
> To be sure there is justification; but justification comes to an end. (#191-2)

I should like now to gather up the loose-ends of the clues provided by the foregoing themes for coming to grips with the central thrust of Wittgenstein's On Certainty. Clearly, he is convinced that Moore is right in his insistence that those who maintain a scepticism with regard to the existence of the external world are deeply confused. At the same time, he is equally convinced that Moore himself fails to realize just how deep this confusion runs. There is something misguided, both about arguing against and about arguing on behalf of such considerations.

It is important to bear in mind that for Wittgenstein the central issue is the broader, or deeper one of what does it mean to doubt or affirm those 'beliefs' which comprise the very framework within which doubting and affirming take place. So, in other words, what is the nature of the certainty that pervades and underminds all language, making it possible to doubt or affirm anything at all? Thus the conclusion to which he comes will have fundamental significance for a wide variety of philosophical topics, including the problem of other minds,

179

the justification of induction, the justification
of moral reasoning, and the possibility of religious knowledge.

All of the themes discussed thus far point
themselves to this more fundamental issue. There
are questions that arise about the epistemological
status of certain bedrock aspects of our experience that cannot be treated in the usual fashion.
It is not helpful to speak of those who cast dis-
paragement on these aspects as 'mistaken', nor is
it helpful to speak of the efforts to defend them
as 'proofs'. Furthermore, Wittgenstein suggests
that knowledge is, after all, based in the language-games through which we originally learned
and by which we continue to experience the world.
Knowing that is not, in the final analysis,
clearly distinguishable from knowing how. What
is needed is a way of understanding the character
of knowledge about bedrock considerations which
is both helpful and in harmony with that character. As Wittgenstein puts it:

> 'But is it an adequate answer to the
> scepticism of the idealist, or the
> assurances of the realist, to say that
> "There are physical objects" is nonsense?
> For them after all it is not nonsense.
> It would, however, be an answer to say:
> this assertion, or its opposite, is a
> misfiring attempt to express what can't
> be expressed like that. And that it
> does misfire can be shown; but that isn't
> the end of the matter. We need to realize
> that what presents itself to us as the
> first expression of a difficulty, or of
> its solution, may not yet be correctly
> expressed at all. Just as one who has
> a just censure of a picture to make will
> often at first offer the censure where
> it does not belong, and an investigation

is needed in order to find the right point of attack for the critic. (#37)

The best clue to Wittgenstein's way of treating epistemological bedrock is found in the above quotation; specifically in the statement that an argument on either side of such questions is a 'misfiring attempt to express what can't be expressed like that. And that it does misfire can be shown'. This statement brings to mind the remark in the Tractatus, "Some things cannot be said; they shew themselves", which serves well as a motto for the "descriptive" nature of the explorations carried out in the Philosophical Investigations. I would suggest that Wittgenstein's main contention in On Certainty is that the character of epistemological bedrock can only be displayed or allowed to show itself; every attempt to doubt it or justify it becomes entangled in self-stultifying confusion. The remainder of this chapter will be devoted to the substantiation and elaboration of this claim.

There are four dominant motifs by means of which Wittgenstein renders his contention that epistemological bedrock cannot be spoken of directly, but only indirectly. One of these motifs is that of allowing such bedrock considerations to 'show' or 'exhibit' themselves in the way we behave, both verbally and non-verbally. In addition to the above quotation, the following remarks make his point quite clearly:

> 'My life shows that I know or am certain that there is a chair over there, or a door, and so on. --I tell a friend e.g. "Take that chair over there", "Shut the door", etc. etc.' (#7)
> 'We need to show that even if he never uses the words "I know...", his conduct exhibits the things we are concerned with.' (#427)

'Am I not getting closer and closer
to saying that in the end logic cannot
be described? You must look at the
practice of language, then you will
see it.' (#501)

A second motif is that of calling attention
to the 'structure/content' character of the relationship between the sort of considerations
being focused on by Moore and the more common
epistemological questions. To put it quite bold-
ly, Wittgenstein maintains that there are some
things which form the framework (structure) for
the very possibility of knowing anything else
(content) at all, and although the various aspects of this framework cannot be doubted, neither can they be 'justified' in the usual sense
of that term. He contends that this 'world-picture' is the 'inherited background against which
I distinguish between true and false'. (#94)
This world-picture functions as a 'mythology'
that provides the structure within which the true-
false game is played, without any explicit reference to the mythology being necessary. Perhaps
the most straight-forward way of putting the matter is the following:

'All testing, all confirmation and dis-
confirmation of a hypothesis takes place
already within a system. And this system is not a more or less arbitrary and
doubtful point of departure for all our
arguments; no, it belongs to the essence
of what we call an argument. The system
is not so much the point of departure, as
the element in which arguments have their
life.' (#105)

The mention of the possible arbitrary nature
of our common epistemological framework brings up
yet another motif in Wittgenstein's way of treating the matter. After all, doesn't this approach

erroneously imply that one could simply choose a different, perhaps conflicting, framework within which to carry on the cognitive enterprise? How, then, is the framework within which we find ourselves living and working to be justified? Wittgenstein's answer is that of course epistemological frameworks are not a matter of choice, but neither are they justified in the standard ways. They are justified, he contends, by bringing to light the part they play in the fabric of our particular 'form of life'. Their 'reasonableness' shows itself in the 'decisions' and 'actions' of human behaviour. (#110) It is misleading to speak as if we choose or assume the various aspects of our epistemological framework, since this way of putting it makes it sound arbitrary and self-conscious when in fact it is not. The viability of bedrock 'beliefs' (if they are to be called that) shows itself in the give-and-take of human existence.

> 'My life shews that I know or am certain
> that there is a chair over there, or a
> door, and so on. --I tell a friend e.g.
> "Take that chair over there","Shut the
> door", etc. etc. (#7)

At times Wittgenstein even speaks of our epistemological framework being grounded in our most primitive 'natural history' or 'animal nature'. (#534-8) The process of induction, for example, no more needs justification than does the squirrel's instinctive gathering of nuts for the winter --its proof is in the eating. Wittgenstein's most forceful presentation of this point is:

> 'I want to regard man here as an animal;
> as a primitive being to which one grants
> instinct but not ratiocination. As a
> creature in a primitive state. Any logic
> good enough for a primitive means of

183

communication needs no apology from us.
Language did not emerge from some kind
of ratiocination.' (#475)

This brings us to the fourth and final motif
in Wittgenstein's rendering of his overall theme.
The grounding of bedrock beliefs in natural history and/or instinctive behaviour would seem to
imply that they are beyond both discussion and
alteration.   The major thrust of this chapter
has been to show that Wittgenstein did not view
such matters as beyond discussion, but rather
that he opted for 'indirect' discussion (in the
form of questions, paradoxical statements, and
metaphoric utterances) by way of allowing bedrock
to bring itself to light.   That he did not maintain that bottom level epistemological considerations are beyond alteration becomes clear from
the following.   It would, indeed, be possible to
'reason' with someone who did not share in the
same framework (though, presumably, it would be
necessary that he shared to some extent in the
same form of life), but such reasoning would be
aimed at 'persuading' him of (not 'demonstrating'
to him) the superiority of one's own world-picture.   The following remarks get right to the
heart of the matter:

'Supposing we met people who did not
regard that as a telling reason.  Now,
how do we imagine this?  Instead of the
physicist, they consult an oracle.  (And
for that we consider them primitive.)  Is
it wrong for them to consult an oracle
and be guided by it?  --If we call this
"wrong" aren't we using our language-
game as a base from which to combat
theirs?'
'And are we right or wrong to combat it?
Of course there are all sorts of slogans
which will be used to support our pro-
ceedings.'

184

'Where two principles really do meet
which cannot be reconciled with one
another, then each man declares the
other a fool and heretic.'
'I said I would "combat" the other
man,--but wouldn't I give him reasons?
Certainly; but how far do they go?  At
the end of reasons comes persuasion.
(Think what happens when missionaries
convert natives. (#609-612)

   Although he speaks negatively of the way in
which we usually characterize those who seem to
operate off of a bedrock different from our own,
it should not be concluded that Wittgenstein
thought 'conversions' from one way of thinking
to another either impossible or unimportant.  He
does, after all, remind us that missionaries do
convert natives and that there is a kind of
'reasoning' which characterizes persuasion that
distinguishes it from coercion and/or conditioning.  The line of demarcation between these concepts may well be difficult to draw, but the
whole point of Wittgenstein's enterprise in On
Certainty has been predicated on the necessity
and possibility of drawing it.  Otherwise, the
distinction between epistemologically primitive
beliefs and other, more common beliefs is of no
value.  For, if the former are reducible, à la
Hume, to mere conditioning, then the latter are
devoid of knowledge as well.  And thus, Wittgenstein's insights themselves would have been impossible.

## 2.  The Notion of Tacit Knowing

   One helpful way of summarizing Wittgenstein's
position in On Certainty is in terms of the concept of 'tacit knowledge'.  In spite of the nervousness often caused by the introduction of such
a concept into serious philosophical considera-

tions, this is precisely the direction in which Wittgenstein's later thought was moving. In brief, he argues: (1) that we can and, indeed, must always know more than we can say; (2) that such knowledge embodies our 'personal backing'; (3) that doubts about bedrock matters are out of place; (4) that the reality and character of the epistemological framework within which we carry on the reasoning enterprise cannot be focused on or articulated explicitly, but reveals itself subsidiarily in our behaviour; (5) that justification of rational procedure can only be given in terms of the commitments which make up our way of being in the words; and (6) that none of these considerations detract from the rationality and/or viability of the search for truth; indeed, they alone make it possible and meaningful.

Anyone familiar with the thought of Michael Polanyi will recognize the essential parallels between it and the above summary of Wittgenstein's later work. For those unfamiliar with Polanyi's thought, the following brief account will illustrate the parallel and substantiate the claim that Wittgenstein's work moves in a direction generally ignored in established philosophical circles.

At the basis of Polanyi's overall position stand the distinctions between focal and subsidiary awareness on the one hand and conceptual and bodily activity on the other. In all cognitive contexts we attend from certain subsidiary factors and to other focal factors. Thus there always are factors which must be taken for granted--for certain--if there is to be any awareness at all. At the same time our involvement in the world is always characterized by both conceptual and bodily activity, each of which carries a cognitive dimension. Now, the interaction between focal awareness and conceptual activity gives rise to explicit knowledge--knowledge characterized by analytic clarity, deductive and/or inductive logic, and 'sayability'. Correspondingly, the interaction between subsidiary awareness and bodily activity gives rise to <u>tacit</u> knowledge--knowledge characterized by the employment of skills, patterns of behaviour, and 'show-ability'. Finally, and most importantly, tacit knowledge is logically prior to explicit knowledge. Thus there must always be some 'truths' whose certainty is beyond or beneath, being made explicit if there is to be any explicit knowledge at all. As Polanyi puts it:

> 'Things of which we are focally aware can be explicitly (sic) identified; but no knowledge can be <u>wholly</u> <u>explicit</u>. For one thing, the meaning of language, when in use, lies in its tacit component; for another, to use language involves actions of our body of which we have only a subsidiary awareness. Hence, tacit knowing is more fundamental than explicit knowing: <u>we</u> <u>can</u> <u>know</u> <u>more</u> <u>than</u> <u>we</u> <u>can</u> <u>tell</u> and <u>we</u> <u>can</u> <u>tell</u> <u>nothing</u> <u>without</u> <u>relying</u> <u>on</u> <u>our</u> <u>awareness</u> <u>of</u> <u>things</u> <u>we</u> <u>may</u> <u>not</u> <u>be</u> <u>able</u> <u>to</u> <u>tell</u>.'[1]

The foregoing system of distinctions offered by Polanyi dovetails nicely with Wittgenstein's concerns in <u>On</u> <u>Certainty</u>. Both are aimed at revealing the fact that some knowledge cannot be said but must show itself, and that attempts to deny and/or defend such certainties always and only result in confusion. For the denial of bedrock certainties--such as the reality of the external world and the rationality of induction--must itself have a place to stand. And the attempt to render such certainties explicit by resorting to arguments which presuppose them is at best superfluous. As Wittgenstein says: 'It is so difficult to find the <u>beginning</u>. Or, better:

187

it is difficult to begin at the beginning.  And
not try to go further back'. (#471)

Another main theme of Polanyi's thought, only touched on in the above remarks, is that of
the importance of bodily activity as the primary
manifestation and basis of tacit knowledge.  He
employs the concept of 'indwelling' in order to
suggest how our most fundamental and pervasive
knowledge is obtained and displayed.  Tacit knowledge is acquired, not through analysis and argument, but by means in imitation, empathy, and
practice.  Thus, it can only be experienced and
evaluated in the skills and behaviour patterns,
the decisions and deeds, which make up our daily
existence.

> 'We know another person's mind by the
> same integrative process by which we
> know life.  A novice trying to under-
> stand the skill of a master, will seek
> mentally to combine his movements to the
> pattern to which the master combines them
> practically.  By such exploratory indwell-
> ing the novice gets the feel of the master's
> skill.  Chess players must enter into a
> master's thought by repeating the games
> he played.  We experience a man's mind as
> the joint meaning of his actions from
> outside.'[2]

This concept of indwelling is helpful in
focusing Wittgenstein's understanding of actions
and decisions as the foundation of the type of
certainty under discussion.  He stresses participation in the active and speaking human community as the child's means of acquiring language and the bedrock 'belief-system' inherent
in it.  This stress is essentially similar to
Polanyi's emphasis on behavioural indwelling,

since it calls attention to the skill-character of the fundamental dimension of cognitivity. Conceptual inderstanding is, for both Wittgenstein and Polanyi, essentially a matter of 'knowing how to go on', 'how to find one's way about'. Polanyi's point is so well summed up in Wittgenstein's comment: 'Knowledge (<u>Wissen</u>) is in the end based on acknowledgement (<u>Anerkennung</u>). (#378)

Another and most important aspect of Polanyi's thought pertains to the worry over the relation of tacit knowledge to relativism, scepticism, and/or fideism. It is often argued that if knowledge is ultimately based on unjustified certainties, then truth is a function of bias, no real knowledge is possible, and one is free to believe whatever one wants. In a word, it is alleged that the concept of tacit knowledge undermines the distinction between responsible and irresponsible belief. However, Polanyi argues that the drive for "universal intent", namely the bedrock "assumption" that all assertions and beliefs seek to be true for all open-minded persons, functions not as a guarantee of truth, but as an adequate means of distinguishing between responsible and irresponsible belief.

'While compulsion by force or by neurotic obsession excludes responsibility, compulsion by universal intent establishes responsibility. The strain of this responsibility is the greater-other things being equal-the wider the range of alternatives left open to choice and the more conscientious the person responsible for the decision.' While the choices in question are open to arbitrary egocentric decision, a craving for the univeral sustains a constructive effort and narrows down this discretion to the point where the agent making the decision finds that he cannot do otherwise. The

freedom of the subjective person to do as
he pleases is overruled by the freedom of
the responsible person to act as he must.[3]

This theme has equally important significance
for Wittgenstein's thought as developed in On
Certainty. He, too, takes special pains to point
out that the bedrock nature of certain ways of
thinking and behaving in no way implies that they
are arbitrary or irrational. Rather, they are
themselves the necessary conditions of rationality.
Furthermore, even when it becomes apparent that a
particular difference of opinion is the result of
language-games which do not overlap, and reasoning shades off into persuasion, persuasion does
take place, and it is not be to confused with cre-
dulity or external compulsion. As long as persons share a common form of life there remain
common features which give rise to a tacit knowledge based not in arbitrariness but in universal
intent.


It should be clear by now that the concept
of tacit knowing, as thus related to Wittgenstein's epistemological posture in On Certainty,
casts considerable light on the question of the
relation between knowledge and language on the
one hand and the reality and structure of the
world on the other. Ever since Kant constructed
his wall between the phenomenal and noumenal
worlds the debate between "idealists" (nee
Rationalists) and "realists" (nee Empiricists)
has centered around the nature of the relationship amongst thought, language, and reality. It
have generally gone unnoticed that both sides of
this debate have assumed (1) that either the
world exists independently of the mind or it is
entirely a function of it, (2) that all knowledge of reality must be explicit, and (3) that
all true statements about the world must be expressed in direct discourse. Wittgenstein's

later work, along with Polanyi's insights, stands in opposition to these assumptions, and when incorporated provides a way of overcoming the dualisms so characteristic of modern philosophy.

By virtue of his stress on metaphorical expression and understanding, Wittgenstein has proposed, albeit indirectly, a perspective from within which (1) the world and the human mind (the known and the knower) stand in a symbiotic relation to one another, each constituting the other, (2) all knowledge cannot be explicit, but must be based in the tacit speech and behavioral patterns which comprise our form of life, and (3) the most appropriate mode of expressing the tacit truths of this most fundamental level of existence is of necessity indirect, or metaphoric, in nature.

3. Mediation and Metaphoric Expression

A notion which serves very well as a means of integrating the foregoing emphases on the symbiotic relationship between language and reality, and logical priority of tacit knowing, and the primordial character of metaphoric speech is that of mediation. I shall conclude this chapter by suggesting how this notion can be used as the axis around which these ontological, epistemological, and linguistic ramifications orbit to provide a meaningful overall perspective. It should be clear that while inspired by the insights offered by Wittgenstein, the following suggestions are in no way to be construed as results of an exegesis of his thought.

Generally speaking reality and thought are envisioned as over-against one another, as existing in different realms, as being "out there" and "in here", respectively. This view has been especially dominant since Kant, and of course it leads to the standard epistemological dichotomies between the knower and the known, between objectivity and subjectivity. To view reality and thought in this dualistic manner gives rise to various forms of Realism and correspondent correspondence theories of truth. To collapse this dualism, à la Hegel, leads to Idealism and coherence theories of truth. A third alternative is to retain the dualism and deny the possibility of bridging the gap between reality and thought; thus skepticism.

The ontological perspective entailed by taking a symbiotic view of the relation between reality and thought is one of relational interactionism or of a process orientation similar to that of Whitehead. In this perspective these two poles of experience mutually constitute one another. Moreover the symbiosis is not a static one wherein the line of demarcation between the poles remains fixed; rather, there is a continual interaction between them which itself becomes the central ontological reality. This interactive nexus is seen as more fundamental than the polar concepts of thought and reality comprised by it.

A helpful way of focusing this ontological perspective is in terms of the notion of mediation. Rather than thinking of reality and thought as standing statically side by side, it is more fruitful to think of them as interpenetrating one another and mediating one another. That is, their respective existence and reality is found in and through, rather than independently of each other. The different aspects and levels of richness of thought and reality can be thought of as dimensions rather than as realms. Dimensions exist simultaneously and are interpenetrated by one another. Moreover the richer or more comprehensive dimensions are mediated in and through the less rich and less comprehensive.

The following passages from Wittgenstein's later work clearly suggest this mediational perspective:

It seems paradoxical to us that we should make such a medley, mixing physical states and states of consciousness up together in a single report: "He suffered great torments and tossed about restlessly". It is quite usual; so why do we find it paradoxical? Because we want to say that the sentence deals with both tangibles and intangibles at once.--But does it worry you if I say: "These three struts give the building stability"? Are three and stability tangible?--Look at the sentence as an instrument, and at its sense as its employment. (#421)

It is possible to say "I read timidity in this face" but at all events the timidity does not seem to be merely associated, outwardly connected, with the face; but fear is there, alive in the features. If the features change slightly, we can speak of a corresponding change in the fear. (#537)

"I noticed that he was out of humour." Is this a report about his behaviour or his state of mind? ("The sky looks threatening": is this about the present or the future?) Both; not side-by-side, however, but about the one via the other. (p. 179)

The world can be viewed, then, as a hierarchy of mutually inter-dependent dimensions, aligned according to a scale of richness, and engaged in an on-going process of interaction. Furthermore, these dimensions mediate one another in that their existence is both determined and expressed only in terms of their inter-relationships. One can think of such dimensions as the physical, the social, the moral, the personal, the aesthetic, and the religious. Each is richer than and inclusive of the former, its reality being dependent on but also transcending those beneath it; each is mediated by but not exhausted by its less comprehensive counterparts. Within each dimension, the poles comprising the "force-field" constituting that dimension, the symbiotic foci of thought and reality, are also mediated in and through each other in that they cannot exist independently.

This notion of mediation also serves as means of relating the tacit basis of knowledge to the ontology sketched above. A mediated reality is one which is experienced and known in-directly, according to a "from-to" pattern. That is to say, the knower attends from - and through - the particulars comprising a more comprehensive dimension, themselves comprised by particulars of less comprehensive dimensions, to its unity or meaning. Thus, even as the reality of the increasingly rich dimensions of experience is mediated through the less rich dimensions, so our knowledge of these dimensions is mediated as well. In other words, as we attend from those particulars of which we are but subsidiarily aware and with which we interact bodily, we come to know their reality and meaning tacitly. Out of this tacit knowledge we can move toward a more explicit knowing, in terms of focal awareness and conceptual precision, but never in such a way as to be able to articulate fully all that we know. The cognitivity dimension of our ex-

istence has a vectorial and thus mediated thrust
to it, even as does the ontological.  Tacit knowledge is of mediated reality.

Wittgenstein speaks of tacit knowing in
terms of "imponderable evidence" in the following generally unnoticed passage from the
Investigations:

It is certainly possible to be convinced by evidence that someone is in
such-and-such a state of mind, that,
for instance, he is not pretending.
But 'evidence' here includes 'imponderable' evidence.
The question is:  what does imponderable
evidence accomplish?
Suppose there were imponderable evidence
for the chemical (internal) structure of
a substance, still it would have to prove
itself to be evidence by certain consequences which can be weighed.
(Imponderable evidence might convince
someone that a picture was a genuine...
But it is possible for this to be proved
right by documentary evidence as well.
Imponderable evidence includes subtle-
ties of glance, of gesture, of tone.
I may recognize a genuine loving look,
distinguish it from a pretended one
(and here there can, of course, be a
'ponderable' confirmation of my judgment).  But I may be quite incapable of
describing the difference.  And this not
because the languages I know have no
words for it.  For why not introduce
new words?--If I were a very talented
painter I might conceivably represent
the genuine and the simulated glance
in pictures.
Ask yourself:  How does a man learn to

get a 'nose' for something?  And how can
this nose be used? (p. 228, part two).

Some examples should help.  The reality and
knowledge of <u>linguistic</u> <u>meaning</u> is mediated on
an ontological level in and through the particulars which comprise it, namely conventional
sounds, grammar, gestures, social context, and
individual intentions.  It is both dependent on
these particulars and transcendent of them in
the sense that it cannot exist without them but
cannot be explained fully in terms of them.  At
the same time each of these particulars, say
grammar, is itself a comprehensive whole whose
reality is mediated in and through the particulars of a less rich dimension, namely word order,
inflection patterns, and punctuation.  In a similar vein, the <u>aesthetic</u> <u>reality</u> of a painting is
mediated and known in and through the particulars
of color, shape, line, texture, and composition,
without being reducible to them.  It both depends
upon them and transcends them.  The reality and
knowledge of <u>persons</u> exhibits this same pattern
of mediation, <u>from</u> and through the particulars
of behavior, appearance, and memory <u>to</u> self and
intention.

This epistemological perspective stands in
direct contrast to the traditional critical views,
whether Empiricist or Rationalist.  Both of these
approaches view knowledge and its attainment exclusively in terms of direct, explicit precision
of definition and inference.  As has been argued
in the previous section, while explicit knowing
is both possible and valuable, it cannot stand
alone but must always be grounded in tacit knowing.  Indirect, informal, and unarticulated
knowledge is logically prior to and provides the
context for direct, formal, and explicit knowledge.

Dimensional reality and tacit knowing share
this mediational character with the metaphoric
mode of expression. Whereas direct discourse is
appropriate to explicit knowledge and unmediated,
physical reality, indirect expression is the
fitting mode for our tacit awareness of the mediated dimensions of reality. That which exists
in mediated relationship and is known tacitly can
only be given expression by means of speech which
suggests and "shows" more than it "says" directly.
The logical priority of the metaphoric mode has
been the primary burden of much of this entire
study, especially of the last chapter. The connections between this primoridality and epistemological bedrock has been the concern of the present chapter. Both the form and content of Wittgenstein's later work provide the pivotal insight
and paradigmatic embodiment for the blending of
these two emphases. The following paragraph
from the Investigations is an excellent example:

> Understanding a sentence is much more
> akin to understanding a theme in music
> than one may think. What I mean is that
> understanding a sentence lies nearer than
> one thinks to what is ordinarily called
> understanding a musical theme. Why is
> just this the pattern of variation in
> loudness and tempo? One would like to
> say "Because I know what it's all about."
> But what is it all about? I should not
> be able to say. In order to 'explain' I
> could only compare it with something
> else which has the same rhythm (I mean
> the same pattern). (One says "Don't you
> see, this is as if a conclusion were be-
> ing drawn" or "This is as it were a paren-
> thesis", etc. How does one justify such
> comparisons?--There are very different
> kinds of justification here.) (#527)

Notes

Chapter Eight

1. Personal Knowledge, (New York: Harper
   Torehboks, 1964), p. x.

2. "The Logic of Tacit Inference", Philosophy,
   Jan. 1966, p. 14

3. Personal Knowledge, p. 309

# Chapter Nine

## --Philosophy As Metaphor--

It is possible to have followed the line of
argument throughout the preceding chapters, and
to be in essential agreement with the interpretation of the later Wittgenstein therein presented, and still to be wondering, "What's it all
worth, philosophically?" It is not uncommon to
encounter philosophers who complain that for all
his provocativeness and genuine insight, Wittgenstein still fails to establish a solid case for
his way of doing philosophy. My own conclusion
is that the primary significance of Wittgenstein's
work for philosophy lies in his suggestion that
at the most fundamental level philosophy is a
metaphorical enterprise. In other words, the
greatest value of his philosophical work is to
force us to rethink what it means to "establish
a solid case" for a philosophical perspective.
In this concluding chapter I shall explore the
ramifications of this aspect of Wittgenstein's
contribution.

### 1.   Philosophy As Conceptual Resolution

There can be little doubt that Wittgenstein
claimed, in his later work, to be proposing a
fresh way of doing philosophy. It will be helpful to begin this chapter with a brief account
of the primary thrust of this proposal. The
difference between his earlier and later writings
is by now quite familiar. It is perhaps best
captured in the following quotation:

"The general form of propositions is: This
is how things are.--That is the kind of proposition that one repeats to oneself count-
less times. One thinks that one is tracing
the outline of the thing's nature over and
over again, and one is merely tracing round
the frame through which we look at it. A
picture held us captive. And we could not
get outside it, for it lay in our language
and language seemed to repeat it to us
inexorably. When philosophers use a word--
"Knowledge", "being", "object", "I", "proposition", "name"--and try to grasp the
essence of the thing, one must always ask
oneself: is the word ever actually used
in this way in the language-game which is
its original home?--What we do is to bring
words back from their metaphysical to
their everyday use." [1]

There is a two-fold contrast drawn in this
quotation, a particular or surface one and a general or deep one. The former is between two views
of the function of language, the picture theory
and the language-game theory. By this time of
day this contrast needs no further elaboration.
The latter contrast is between two different ways
of doing philosophy, two different "pictures" or
models of what constitutes the philosophic enterprise. The first is what Wittgenstein calls the
"metaphysical", the approach which sees philosophy as a sort of super-science aiming at the
"essence" of things through the examination of
concepts. The second is what is best termed a
functional model, the approach which views philosophy as conceptual clarification through the
exploration of everyday speech.

What is important to note for the purposes
of this chapter is that each of these ways of
doing philosophy is itself a model or metaphor,

202

and is usually presented as such in the writings of those philosophers who subscribe to it. The metaphysical posture has been based primarily on metaphors drawn from deductive systems, such as mathematics and law, and inductive systems, such as empirical science. The functional posture is based primarily on metaphors drawn from the pragmatic and social dimensions of human existence.

Moreover, it is essential to grasp the fact that not only are the major ways of doing philosophy themselves grounded in metaphor, but the very criteria by means of which we are urged to judge the merits of these approaches to philosophy are metaphorically based as well. In other words, there are no criteria for adjudicating amongst basic metaphorical postures which are themselves "objective" in the sense of being devoid of metaphorical anchorage. And from this realization two things follow. First, that the assumption that there are objective criteria by means of which metaphors can be confirmed or disconfirmed is itself part and parcel of a particular metaphorical view, namely that of modern positivism. Second, that this state of affairs does not lead necessarily to some form of "hard-nose" relativism and/or skepticism.

Those who have perpetrated the fairy tale of the necessity and actuality of totally objective criteria--and this includes the vast majority of modern thinkers--have been guilty of carrying a good thing too far. In their zeal to overcome the obvious limitations and evils of criteria which were at the beck and call of various vested interests, be they social or personal, modern thinkers have constructed a monster of their own, one which is inherently more detrimental than those it was designed to offset. For the modern view creates the illusion that purely objective criteria exist, thereby eliminating by fiat any possibility of discussion and/or self-criticism at the fundamental level.

The only alternative to the "cult of objectivity" is not relativistic subjectivism. A more viable line of approach is to recognize that we live in a conversation among the personal, the social, and the physical dimensions of reality, and that each of these dimensions exerts its pull upon us in a specific historical context. As human beings we struggle to maintain our balance in this constantly fluctuating situation, and because of individual and cultural differences we do this in somewhat different ways. We find different models or metaphors by means of which to chart our courses. Nevertheless, there are certain commonalities which comprise the human form of life and which may be thought of as forming the bedrock or touchstone for evaluating the overall worth of our chosen models.

Now, the difference between this alternative and that of objectivism is that while the latter maintains it is possible to articulate explicitly the character of these bedrock criteria, the present view does not. It contends, rather, that while these bedrock features of existence are shared in by all humans, they cannot be focused directly as specific criteria or "truths" without violating their nature. For whatever can be so focused and articulated can no longer be bedrock in character, since we must be attending from something in order to attend to something else and that which is attended from is what is bedrock. Thus the necessity of expressing such bedrock criteria exclusively by means of the indirect, metaphoric mode. The various metaphors developed to deal with any aspect of experience at any point in time are judged according to what might be called "experiential fit", rather than by supposed objective criteria on the one hand or by strictly subjective factors on the other. [2]

The appropriateness of Wittgenstein's insights to all these should now become clear. By implication in the _Investigations_, and explicitly in _On Certainty_, both the substantive thrust and the method of presentation of Wittgenstein's later work depend directly upon the view of the relation between metaphor and knowledge sketched above. Not only does he maintain that metaphoric expression runs deeper than propositional expression, but his method of presentation is itself metaphorical in nature. In a word, he doesn't present "knock-down, drag-out arguments" for his view, _because_ his view is that such arguments do not cut deep enough. Thus what it means to establish a solid case for a philosophy, especially when engaged in metaphilosophy, has in Wittgenstein's work been redefined. His is a philosophy "by invitation" in the sense that we are being asked to explore our philosophic posture and concerns by means of a fresh set of metaphors to see if they are not helped considerably thereby.

More specifically, Wittgenstein relies most heavily upon the metaphoric mode, especially as it constitutes the heart of everyday speech, because it is at the practical level of existence that we are closest to the bedrock of our form of life. At this level the most fundamental "truths" of our existence _show_ themselves in the ways we behave and in the indirect ways we express ourselves, even though they cannot be _said_ in propositional form. Everyday speech, which is heavily flavored with and grounded in metaphor, is the necessary "ground-zero' or 'square one" of both our life and our thought. Thus whatever theories we articulate at the abstract level-- whether they be about minds, matter, meaning, or truth--must grow out of and be judged by the metaphors and dynamics of concrete, everyday speech.

An entirely different way of stating the central thrust of Wittgenstein's proposal for philosophy might run like this. Without too much oversimplification it can be said that traditionally philosophers have viewed philosophical problems as having definite answers, and thus as being capable of being <u>solved</u>. The history of philosophy is often seen as the history of the various answers and theses offered by philosophers as solutions to philosophical problems. At the beginning of the Twentieth Century the picture of the function of philosophy underwent radical change. While some thinkers, such as Bertrand Russell, still maintained that philosophical problems must be solved--though Russell did argue for a new method of arriving at solutions, namely the method of mathematical logic--many other thinkers, represented by both J.J. Ayer and the young Wittgenstein, came to regard philosophical problems as "pseudo-problems" which cannot be solved, but only <u>dissolved</u>. The only problems capable of solution, according to such logical empiricists, are those which lie in the domains of the various sciences. Philosophy's function is simply to distinguish between the "real-problems" (scientific and logical ones) and the "pseudo-problems".

Now, it is often thought--even among people who should surely know better--that the later Wittgenstein shared this view that philosophical problems and/or metaphysical problems are not to be solved, but only dissolved. While he does direct many of his remarks against the views of traditional philosophers and Russell, a careful reading of the <u>Philosophical Investigations</u> should make it clear that Wittgenstein does <u>not</u> maintain that philosophical problems are psuedo-problems, only capable of being dissolved. My own suggestion is that a more profitable way to characterize his view of philosophical problems is to say that rather than maintaining either that they are to be solved or that they are to be dissolved, Wittgenstein contends that philosophical problems are to be <u>resolved</u>.  The point of putting it this way is three-fold:  first, the resolution of a problem, unlike the dissolution of a problem, implies that the problem is (or was) real; second, this way of speaking still distinguishes philosophical problems from scientific ones which have specific answers; and third, the term 'resolution' suggests the sort of conceptual and linguistic disentanglement which characterizes Wittgenstein's actual procedure.  Knots are untied (solved), fake knots are exposed (dissolved), but tangles are disentangled (resolved).

> The problems are solved, not by giving new information, but by arranging what we have always known.  Philosophy is a battle against the bewitchment of our intelligence by means of language. (#109)

Paragraph number 109 serves as an excellent summary or thesis statement of Wittgenstein's position on the function of philosophy.  It contains essentially three contentions, around which the remarks comprising the paragraphs of this unit of the <u>Investigations</u> (nos. 109-133) are centered. Wittgenstein's first emphasis is that philosophical considerations are unlike those of science, since they do not admit of being stated as empirical hypotheses.  Philosophical considerations are conceptual and linguistic, and therefore do not yield answers which can be classified as information in the storehouse of knowledge.  The inconclusiveness of the history of philosophy might be offered as evidence of the truth of this contention.  Whatever philosophy is, it is not science.  Wittgenstein would direct these remarks against Russell's view of philosophy as well-philosophy is not a "super-science" (cf.no.97).

Since scientific considerations are the sorts of things which seek and yield explanations, philosophy cannot be thought to deal with explaining anything.

The second emphasis of paragraph no. 109 is positive in nature. Though philosophy does not deal in providing explanations, it can be said to concern itself with descriptions. Descriptions of what? Descriptions of the way concepts and linguistic utterances are used in the business of everyday life ("the workings of our language"). The point here seems to be that because we are so familiar with the workings of our language, we often fail to recognize them for what they are, and hence allow ourselves to become entangled in a hopeless confusion of categories. As long as we use language for its ordinary purpose, there are no difficulties which cannot be handled by the further use of ordinary language ("everything is in order as it is"; no. 98). However, when we begin to analyze our language and concepts, we are often misled into thinking that we are explaining them. As Wittgenstein puts it in paragraph no. 38, "Philsophical problems arise when language "goes on holiday" (or "idles"). Thus philosophy must limit itself to a description of how concepts and utterances function. The business of reminding ourselves of the familiar workings of language is a service which is not tobe belittled, given our propensity to get tangled up when we forget them.

The third element in Wittgenstein's thesis paragraph is focused in the contention that "philosophy is a battle against the bewitchment of our intelligence by means of language". The job of philosophy is presented as that of preventing and resolving the misunderstandings which occur when thinkers in any field of endeavor attempt to provide explanatory, rather than descriptive, understanding of conceptual and linguistic activity. Thus the philosophy, far from having defined himself out of a job, or from having reduced philosophy to the task of telling others what they cannot say, has ensured himself of a function which is of universal and lasting value. As long as people talk about talk and thought, and thereby stand in danger of having their intelligence bewitched by language, the philosopher is in business.

We come now to the paragraph (no. 133) in which Wittgenstein focuses most directly upon the question of the aim of philosophy.

> It is not our aim to refine or complete the system of rules for the use of our word in unheard-of-ways.
> For the clarity that we are aiming at is indeed <u>complete</u> clarity.
> But this simply means that the philosophical problems should completely disappear.
> The real discovery is the one that makes me capable of stopping doing philosophy when I want to.--The one that gives philosophy peace, so that it is no longer tormented by questions which bring <u>itself</u> in question.--Instead, we now demonstrate a method, by examples; and the series of examples can be broken off.--Problems are solved (difficulties eliminated), but not a <u>single</u> problems.
> There is not <u>a</u> philosophical method, though there are indeed methods, like different therapies.

It is correct to say that Wittgenstein's approach to philosophy does aim at completeness, but there are different kinds of completeness. First off, there is that which consists in an

exhaustive system of rules for all possible
linguistic uses.  Such would be the completeness
sought by those who construct artificial and
idealized languages.  Secondly, there is that
type of completeness which consists in having a
clear (or full) view of what lies before one at
a given moment.  Such is the completeness sought
by Wittgenstein.  To say it once again, the aim
of philosophy is neither the solving nor the dis-
solving of problems by means of linguistic ana-
lysis--rather it is the resolving of difficulties by means of getting clear about the ways in
which various concepts and utterances function.

The type of completeness Wittgenstein has
in mind does away with the specific philosophical problem in question--by resolving it--but it
does not do away with all philosophical problems
in one fell swoop.  Though he subscribed to the
latter position in his _Tractatus_, in the _Investi-
gations_ Wittgenstein is content to take up specific problems and deal with them one by one.
Such a procedure is one which in one sense will
never be completed, but which in another sense
can be completed at any time--namely, when a
given difficulty has been resolved.  This view of
the function of philosophy provides peace because we are no longer driven by the unrealizable
goal of arriving at an exhaustive and final system of truth about reality.  The use of the con-
tinuous present tense ("stopping doing philosophy") brings this point out clearly.  On the
other hand, there is always plenty of philosophical work to be done--the problems have not
been put aside as pseudo-problems.  Thus, specific difficulties can be dealt with by means of
examples and clear vision, without resorting to
philosophical dogmatism of either the traditional or the positivist type.

Later on (no. 309) Wittgenstein says his
task is that of "showing the fly the way out of

the fly-bottle". The intent of this metaphor is in harmony with the interpretation developed in the preceding paragraphs. Being trapped is a difficulty which does not have a single solution, nor is it a difficulty which can be described as illusory of "pseudo". Showing someone the way out of a trap is not a matter of providing precise rules, but is rather a matter of manipulating the factors involved so as to provide a clear view of how the person got into the trap in the first place. All traps cannot be treated in the same way, nor can all "trapees" be released in the same way. Each must be dealt with contextually.

In the last line of paragraph no. 133. Wittgenstein denies that there is any one method of doing philosophy. Rather, there are many methods in the same way as there are many types of therapy. Here again, in addition to the contribution this remark makes to an understanding of his overall position concerning philosophy, one sees Wittgenstein's uneasiness about all attempts to assimilate one activity to another. Furthermore, the comparison between philosophy and therapy reminds one of the remark in paragraph no. 255: "The philosopher's treatment of a question is like the treatment of an illness." Such treatment cannot be undertaken according to strict rules--though there are, to be sure, rules of thumb--nor can it proceed as if the illness were a "pseudo-illness". Diseases and "mental cramps" are treated individually through relieving the tension created by the lack of harmony among normal physiological or psychological functions.

The foregoing summary of Wittgenstein's "new picture" of the nature of philosophy re-emphasizes the three-fold character of his involvement with metaphor. Not only does he (1) advocate the analysis of ordinary language, the

very fabric of which is comprised of metaphor, as
the chief function of philosophy, but he (2)
couches his case in the metaphoric mode as well.
Moreover, (3) Wittgenstein rests content with
this mode of expression as a means, if not the
means, of making philosophical mileage. His use
and view of metaphor thus entail the viability
of conceiving of philosophy as a metaphoric
enterprise.

## 2. Some Parallel Practitioners

While his work may serve as an outstanding
example of the posture which views philosophy as
a metaphoric enterprise, there is a variety of
directions in which to look for corroboration of
Wittgenstein's proposal. In this section I shall
briefly present the positions of three thinkers
who in one way or another share Wittgenstein's
high regard for the philosophic significance of
metaphor.

Although John Wisdom has been strongly in-
fluenced by Wittgenstein's work, he has also developed many insights and lines of thought which
are distinctly his own. While not addressing
himself exclusively to metaphor as such, Wisdom
presents a case for the philosophic integrity
of ways of speaking which seem especially "odd"
or paradoxical. The overall thesis of Wisdom's
position is that odd-talk is frequently necessary,
both as a means to communicate and as a means to
discover truth. Although he does not argue for
the wholesale acceptance of all odd-talk, Wisdom
does argue for a sympathetic and exploratory
approach to all such talk. Moreover, he maintains that odd-talk is not limited to nonscien-
tific discourse. "I am urging that there is
more of poetry in science and more of science in
poetry than our philosophy permits us readily to
grasp." 3

212

The first theme in Wisdoms' Paradox and
Discovery pertains to the nature of metaphorical language.  Along with Max Black, Wisdom
maintains that far from being odd or dispensable,
metaphorical language is very common and essential to the cognitive function of language in
general.  He focuses on the concrete case of a
woman finally deciding not to purchase a hat because while she was trying to make up her mind a
friend said, "My dear, it's the Taj Mahal."
Against those who would argue that such a statement only influences the hearer's noncognitive
feelings about the hat and can be reduced to
statements about the hat being "like" the Taj
Mahal, Wisdom says:

> My answer is this:  In the first place
> it isn't true that the words about the
> hat only influence the hearer's feelings
> to the hat.  They alter her apprehension
> of the hat just as the word "A hare"makes
> what did look like a clump of earth look
> like an animal, a hare in fact; just as
> the word "A cobra" may change the look
> of something in the corner by the bed.
> It is just because in these instances
> words change the apprehension of what
> is already before one that I refer to
> them.
> Again it isn't true that the words "It's
> the Taj Mahal" meant "It is like the Taj
> Mahal."  This more sober phrase is an
> inadequate substitute.  This reforma-
> tion is a failure.  It's feebler than
> the original and yet it's still too
> strong.  For the hat isn't like the
> Taj Mahal, it's much smaller and the
> shape is very different.  And the still
> more sober substitute "It is in some
> respects like the Taj Mahal" is still
> more inadequate.  It's much too feeble.

> Everything is like everything in some
> respects--a man like a monkey, a mon-
> key like a mongoose, a mongoose like
> a mouse, a mouse like a micro-organism,
> and a man after all is an organism too.
> Heaven forbid that we should say there
> are no contexts in which it is worth
> while to remark this sort of thing.
> But it is not what the woman in the hat
> shop remarked.  What she said wasn't the
> literal truthlike "It's a cobra" said of
> what is, unfortunately, a cobra.  But
> what she said revealed the truth. [4]

This tendency among contemporary philosophers to dismiss odd-talk as meaningless is even
stronger with respect to paradoxical language
than it is with respect to metaphorical language.
The relation between paradox and truth is the
second of Wisdom's major themes.  Wisdom maintains that paradoxical language often leads to
a new and deeper understanding of experience
and reality.  Perhaps the most extreme case of
a paradoxical use of language (as distinguished
from a paradoxical statement) is irony.  When
a statement is made ironically its meaning is in
direct contradiction with what is said.  To use
Austin's terms, its illocutionary force is at
odds with its locutionary force.  In irony the
speaker says the exact opposite of what he means
--yet he expects his meaning to be understood!
Not only is the ironic use of language paradoxical, but the language used to talk about its
paradoxical nature is also paradoxical.  Witness
the above perfectly understandable statement
that in irony one says the opposite of what he
means.

Wisdom traces the empiricists's nervousness
in the face of paradoxical language to two
sources.  One is simply the failure to comprehend
the point that is made by such language, and this

may in turn be based on a legitimate intellectual difficulty.  Another source is the concern
to avoid being victimized by misleading or meaningless confusion.  Although he agrees that a
good deal of caution and rational analysis is
always in order, Wisdom also maintains that

> Such fear, such obsessional fear, of any
> concept which begins to be not quite it-
> self may indeed join with inadequate com-
> prehension of such eccentricity to cramp
> our power to conceive the conceivable.
> For it is with words mainly that we delin-
> eate the conceivable and if we never allow
> words to be a little eccentric, never
> allow ourselves to apply a word to any
> state of affairs actualy or conceivable,
> to which it would not customarily be
> applied, we are without means to refer
> to any state of affairs for which there
> is not yet a word, any possibility un-
> dreamt of in our philosophy.[5]

Wisdom's third theme presents itself in his
attitude towards metaphysical language.  He
thinks that a healthy respect for metaphor and
paradox should render one much less critical of
the sort of thing metaphysically inclined philosophers are prone to say.  There is, of course,
an important distinction to be drawn between
what metaphysicians say when they are doing
their work and what they may say about what
they are doing.  This is an important distinction with respect to any discipline.  The prac-
titioner is often the least reliable theoreti-
cian, in science and mathematic as well as in
art.  Space will not permit a detailed account
of Wisdom's analysis of the function of metaphysical discourse, but the following quotation
should point up the core of his approach:

I believe that if, faced with the extraordinary pronouncements of metaphysicians, we avoid asking them to define their terms, but instead press them to present us with instances of what they refer to contrasted with instances of what they do not refer to, then their pronouncements will no longer appear either as obvious falsehoods or mysterious truths or pretentious nonsense, but as often confusingly presented attempts to bring before our attention certain not fully recognized and yet familiar features of how in the end questions of different types are met. [6]

On the basis of the foregoing emphasis, Wisdom suggests, as yet a fourth theme, that theological discourse can be recalled from the exile to which it was banished by overly eager empiricist philosophers. Once again it must be stressed that such a view does not imply the acceptance of every religious or theological statement as meaningful. It simply implies that each such statement must be dealt with individually within the immediate and broader context wherein it occurs. Wisdom puts it emphatically:

One might have expected that in the sphere of religion everyone would have learned by now to move carefully and neither at once to accept nor hastily to reject what sounds bewildering. But no, even here we still find a tendency to reject strange statements with impatience, to turn from them as absurd or unprovable or to write them down as metaphor--deceptive or at best merely picturesque. Only a few months ago someone came to me troubled about the old but bewildering statement that Christ was both God and man. He had asked those

216

who taught him theology how this could
be true.  Their answers had not satis-
fied him.  I was not able to tell him
what the doctrine means.  But I did remind
him that although some statements which
seem self-contradictory are self-contradictory others are not, that indeed some
of the most preposterous statements ever
made have turned out to convey the most
tremendous discoveries. [7]

Empiricism itself has spawned some of the
best critics of its own narrow view of the cognitive significance of metaphor.  The pragmatic
flavor of W.V.C. Quine's critique is well known,
but perhaps the most thorough reconstruction of
empiricism from within is Alan Pasch's Experience and the Analytic.  One purpose of his detailed and valuable study is to establish that
contemporary empiricism has focused its attention on the analysis of sensory experience, to
the extent that it has completely ignored other
aspects.  Even more important, Pasch maintains
that two main notions employed by contemporary
empiricism, i.e. the analytic/synthetic distinctions and the primacy of sense-data, seriously
distort experience when applied in an a priori
and rigid fashion.  He thinks these notions are
valid when used in a pragmatic and contextual
fashion, but such a use necessitates a great
deal of tolerance with regard to the theories
of meaning, knowledge, and truth.

The first part of Pasch's work is devoted
to a discussion of the importance and nature of
the analytic/synthetic distinction within empiricist thought.  After indicating the centrality
of this distinction in the theories of Hume,
Kant, and contemporary empiricists like C.L.
Lewis, Pasch spends two chapters establishing
the fact that this distinction can only be maintained in a contextual sense.  That is to say,

no absolute basis can be given for making this distinction because it is entirely dependent upon the definitions and rules of any given language context, and since contexts are highly dependent upon individual and social purposes, the distinction is seen to have a pragmatic basis. The only situations in which the distinction holds rigidly, and in which concrete examples can be worked out, are situations in which the context has been defined rigidly in terms of precise definitions and procedural rules.

Such rigidity is found only with in the confines of pure mathematics and artificial languages such as those developed by Bertrand Russell and Rudolph Carnap. Ordinary language and experience do not admit to such rigidity of structure. Thus the result of an empiricism based upon a rigid analytic/synthetic distinction is an empiricism that moves further and further away from experience. In fact, Pasch maintains that this type of empiricism actually degenerates into a form of rationalism, and a study of the language theories of the majority of contemporary empiricists will substantiate this extremely ironic conclusion. Pasch concludes that one can speak of "internal" rigidity in connection with the analytic'synthetic distinction, but that the variety and complexity of ordinary language and experience demand a more tolerant and contextual approach.

> An investigation of the extensional concepts of definition, synonymy, and the distinction between logical and nonlogical terms and statements yielded no positive results so far as a basis for distinguishing between analytic and synthetic truths is concerned, and the conclusion seemed inescapable that this distinction, as well as the concepts that might otherwise have supported it,

must either be defined on the basis of a convention, or else must be said to be a matter of degree. The relations among these concepts of convention and degree I was able to delineate roughly by means of two other concepts: context and the distinction between internal and external questions. Within a well-defined context established by means of conventions, the distinctions between analytic and synthetic and between logical and nonlogical, as well as the collateral ideas of definition and synonymy, are precise concepts, and questions about them are internal questions. Without such a context the concepts are all vague unless entertained as matters of degree, and questions about them are external questions. [8]

The second part of Pasch's book deals with theories of perception which have been developed by contemporary empiricism. Here, too, he accuses empiricism of setting up rigid categories, à la rationalism, that distort perceptual experience and ignore other important aspects of experience. No absolute distinction can be maintained between "the given" of experience and "the categories" of the mind, the atomism of Russell and Lewis and the sense-datum theories of Locke, Hume, and H.H. Price not withstanding. What is "given" for one person in one situation may not be so given for another person, or in another situation. To chop up experience into little atoms, molecules, or sense-date is simply to fly in the face of the fact that experience comes with a variety of relations and contexts, and thus must be considered from a "holistic" perspective.

Pasch suggests that a situational approach to perceptual and cognitive experience is the only one that is both epistemologically and psychologically sound. Such an approach of necessity must consider an individual's needs, purposes, and values in order to do full justice to all the factors of experience. These "subjective" factors influence our perceptions and rational processes as much as do so-called "objective" sensory factors. Experience thus comes on continua between such foci as perception and conception, informality and formality, acting and thinking, and subjectivity and objectivity. Any point on these complex continua may be focused on for a specific purpose, but it must always be remembered that such a focus is functional and flexibly in nature, and neither a priori nor absolute.

> As the gap between the ordinary and the technical kinds of significance becomes wider and empirical significance becomes more of a problem, philosophic attempts to meet the problem becomes more sophisticated, tend to ignore the ordinary kind of significance, and result in a further widening of the gap. The present account may be understood as seeking to restore the experientially prior kind of significance to philosophic empiricism without losing whatever benefits have been won through concern for a rigid criterion of meaning. The vehicle for the restoration is the contextualist theory of significance, which not only prevents the extreme rigidity that leads to suspension of judgment in dealing with empirical contexts but also given rise to a philosophic concept of significance that does justice to and is continuous with experienced significance. The concept of significance emerging from a contextualist approach is continuous with experienced significance because the latter is contextual, and rigidity is prevented because

a contextualist theory is plural-
istic, adapting its criteria to whatever context is to be evaluated. [9]

Part three of Pasch's book is given over to
a summary of the implications of the foregoing
analysis, and to an outline of his own suggested
solution, "pragmatic reconstruction." He states
that a theory of meaning cannot be limited to
the analysis of statements or propositions,
which ignores contextual relations, nor can it
be saddled with a "monolithic" model such as
Quine's, which ignores the flexibility and open
texture of language. In line with Wittgenstein,
Pasch contends that meaning depends on context,
and context depends on purpose and function. In
this way he "stretches" empiricism back to its
original and experiential posture, along the
lines suggested by William James' notion of
"radical empiricism." Now such factors as needs
and values play a significant role in determining
the truth value of various interpretations of
experience. Even metaphysical "hypotheses" become relevant for empirical investigation, provided they are offered in an open-ended way,
and are understood as analogical, parabolic, and
metaphorical models, rather than as descriptive
models. Truth, according to Pasch, is based on
intersubjectivity as a middle-ground between subjective, phenomenalistic solipsism on one side,
and objective, rationalistic certainty on the
other.

Near the end of his book, Pasch mentions
two other thinkers who have proposed interpretations of philosophy which bear positive relation to his own proposal. One is Stephen
Pepper,[10] whose "root metaphor" theory sees
philosophic positions as beginning with seminal
insights which are expanded so as to become
"world hypotheses", aiming at correlating all
dimensions of experience. The other thinker

is Dorothy Emmet,[11] who conceives of metaphysics as essentially an analogical enterprise. The point at which all of these approaches meet, and at which they corroborate the view which sees philosophy as a metaphoric endeavor, is in their insistence that at the most fundamental level the reasoning process is grounded in factors which are no less rational for being insusceptible to precise definition and verificational analysis.

A more recent thinker who has created a great deal of debate in philosophic circles, as a result of his theory of scientific knowledge, is Thomas Kuhn. Kuhn's particular epistemological posture is exceedingly germane to our discussion of philosophy as metaphor, and thus warrants a brief exposition. Moreover, in spite of the parallels between his view and that of Wittgenstein, Kuhn differs from Wittgenstein at the crucial juncture, and this difference is highly instructive vis à vis the clarification of the latter's position.

Kuhn's view of scientific knowledge is built on the idea of a paradigm. He defines paradigms as "accepted examples of actual scientific practice - examples which include law, theory, application, and instrumentation together - providing models from which spring particular coherent traditions of scientific research."[12] Paradigms provide the scientist with his interpretive schema, the pivotal and unquestioned presuppositions of his knowledge and the "facts" of his world. "Normal science", as Kuhn terms it, does not test alternative paradigms but only the puzzles arising from commitment to any particular paradigm.

"Mopping-up operations are what engage most scientists throughout their careers. They constitute what I am here calling

222

normal science. Closely examined, whether historically or in the contemporary laboratory, that enterprise seems an attempt to force nature into the preformed and relatively inflexible box that the paradigm supplies. No part of normal science is to call forth new phenomena; indeed those that will not fit the box are often not seen at all. Nor do scientists normally aim to invent new theories, and they are often intolerant of those invented by others. Instead, normal-scientific research is directed to the articulation of those phenomena and theories that the paradigm already supplies." [13]

Kuhn points out that the working out of the puzzles entailed within a paradigm always leads to certain anomalies which, if significant enough, may produce a crisis for the paradigm. The puzzle-solving process of "normal science" clashes with these anomalies, and then the latter can no longer be ignored or resolved without serious revision of the paradigm, the atmosphere is ripe for a scientific revolution, for what Kuhn calls "extraordinary science."

However, the proposal of the new paradigm, which resolves the tension at the point of crisis, offers no guarantee for a more comprehensive or systematic articulation of the world than the old paradigm. The switch to a new paradigm occurs, not on the basis of empirical evidence but because of some so-called "subjective" factors within the scientific community. Kuhn speaks of these factors alternatively as "Gestalt switches", "conversion experiences", and "persuasion." Since there is no initial evidence that the new paradigm will explain the world any better than the old paradigm, except at the point of crisis,

there is little point in maintaining that the new
paradigm is closer to the truth or is more adequate than the old one. "We may, to be more precise, have to relinquish the notion, explicit or
implicit, that changes of paradigm carry scientists and those who learn from them closer and
closer to the truth." [14]

Thus in Kuhn's view, a view which is often
termed "conventionalism", the history of science
is not a cumulative progression of ever greater
approximation to the truth, but it is, rather, a
history of the embracing of a series of mutually
exclusive paradigms which are nothing more than
alternative ways of seeing the world. According
to Kuhn, progress in science can be made only
when the members of the community have an agreed-
upon-paradigm, for it is the paradigm which actually determines the community's view of the structure and content of the world. Because commitment to a paradigm is a total "way of seeing",
"differences between successive paradigms are
both necessary and irreconcilable." [15] Thus
Kuhn concludes that debates about the relative
merits of competing paradigms are always at cross-
purposes with one another. Because of their all-
encompassing nature, paradigms are logically incommensurable with one another, and since it is
impossible to do science outside of a particular
paradigm, there is no way to adjudicate between
them vis à vis the world.

As we have seen, a paradigm operates as a
very broad interpretive schema, giving meaning
to our experience of the world. Under the epistemological umbrella provided by the paradigm,
no neutral, uninterpreted facts about the world
exist. Paradigm shifts are not, according to
Kuhn, merely reorganizations of the facts comprising the world. They are entirely different
ways of constituting and structuring the world,

including its "facts". "When paradigms change, the world itself changes with them." 16 Thus the justification of a paradigm cannot be based on the criterion of approximation to the truth about the world, because the world as we know it is itself a dependent function of the paradigm.

After having argued against the possibility of viewing science as a progressively more adequate approximation of the truth about reality, and after having shown that paradigms are at once inherently incommensurable and all-inclusive, Kuhn sees no alternative other than to postulate an epistemological relativism. For him there simply is no way to explain or justify rationally the shift from one paradigm to another, since paradigms themselves provide the criteria for scientific rationality. Although he acknowledges the importance of "persuasion" and "translation" in the conversion from one paradigm to another, Kuhn concludes that these techniques are neither sufficient nor necessary, that in the final analysis conversion is a kind of mystery.

> Since translation, if pursued, allows the participants in a communication breakdown to experience vicariously something of the merits and defects of each other's points of view, it is a potent tool both for persuasion and for conversion. But even persuasion need not succeed, and, if it does, it need not be accompanied or followed by conversion. The two experiences are not the same...

> The conversion experience that I have linked to a gestalt switch remains, therefore, at the heart of the revolutionary process. Good reasons for choice provide motives for conversion and a

climate in which it is more likely
to occur.  Translation may, in addition, provide points of entry for the
neural reprogramming that, however
inscrutable at this time, must underlie
conversion.  But neither good reasons
nor translation constitute conversion,
and it is that process we must expli-
cate in order to understand an essential sort of scientific change. [17]

There are two main themes in Kuhn's work
which are highly relevant to the concerns of this
chapter.  The first is the cruciality and comprehensiveness of the notion of paradigm.  The second is the question of logical incommensurability
amongst paradigms.  The former theme runs strongly parallel to the general notion of philosophy
as metaphor and is clearly in harmony with Wittgenstein's emphases in On Certainty.  The latter
theme is one on which Kuhn and Wittgenstein take
opposing positions.

Those who have followed the progression of
thought developed over the last three and a half
chapters should have no difficulty seeing the
parallels between Kuhn's suggestions concerning
the nature of scientific reasoning at the bedrock level and Wittgenstein's position concerning the nature of philosophicla reasoning.  The
notion of paradigm is closely related to that of
metaphor.  Both are conceived, as it were, "on
the job", both provide the framework for patterns
of thought, and both function as the final court
of appeal for interpretive judgments within the
framework they provide.  Thus both serve as bedrock in their respective fields.  A minor difference exists in the sense that Kuhn's notion
of paradigm seems to lie mid-way between the
everyday notion of metaphor employed, and to
some extent explicated, by Wittgenstein on the
one hand and the "deep structure" notion of

226

metaphor, as comprising our way-of-being-in-the-world, on the other hand. Paradigms would seem to be exchanged less often than metaphor in the former sense and more often than in the latter sense.

A major difference, nonetheless, remains between the approaches of Kuhn and Wittgenstein with respect to the idea of incommensurability. Wittgenstein is frequently interpreted as proposing a conventionalist and/or relativist view (often know as "Wittgensteinian Fideism"), wherein worldviews, whether individual or cultural, are based exclusively in sub-rational, subjective factors. Such an interpretation leaves little or no difference between his view and that of Kuhn. My own reading of Wittgenstein, however, does not support this interpretation, as the presentations in Chapters Three and Five make clear.

What those who interpret Wittgenstein in this way, and Kuhn as well, overlook is that the processes of persuasion involved in paradigm and metaphor exchanges themselves have a basis in our human form of life as an activity; a basis which is neither rational nor irrational in the narrow sense of the terms, but which must be designated "reasonable" in the broad sense. There are, after all, patterns of persuasion, justification, and exploration which comprise the warp and weft of our existence, including our standard canons of rational discourse and evaluation, and which thus run deeper. These patterns provide a grounding for our paradigms, and thus in a profoundly pragmatic way they provide the means for exchanging old paradigms for new ones. And these patterns can only be expressed metaphorically, never directly as scientific theories or philosophies.

Thus "objective absolutism" and "subjective conventionalism" are not the only alternatives. Their respective concerns come together in a helpful way when reasoning, whether scientific or philosophic, is seen as an activity <u>within</u> the fabric of human life, a fabric indirectly but sufficiently expressed in the deep metaphors which govern our activity. As Barry Stroud puts it:

> The point of Wittgenstein's examples of people who do not "play our game" is only to show that our having the concepts and practices we have is dependent upon certain facts which might not have obtained. They show only that "the formation of concepts different from the usual ones" is intelligible to us; but it does not follow from this that those concepts themselves are intelligible to us. And since the intelligibility of alternative concepts and practices is required by the thesis of radical conventionalism...I think that thesis is not borne out by Wittgenstein's examples...To ask whether our human practices or forms of life themselves are "correct" or "justified" is to ask whether we are "correct" or "justified" in being the sorts of things we are. [18]

## 3. Concluding Remarks

This brings the present undertaking to a
temporary resting place. I have sought to focus
the implications of Wittgenstein's pervasive
employment of metaphor in relation to the contemporary discussion over the nature of metaphoric
speech as a mode of expression. I have concluded
that not only did Wittgenstein view the metaphoric mode as important and to a large degree
constitutive of our world, but that he saw it as
a means of transcending the traditional epistemological debate between subjectivism and objectivism. Moreover, I submit that Wittgenstein embodied and affirmed an understanding of philosophy as essentially a metaphoric activity, and
that his own explorations stand as an invitation
to think of and practice philosophy in this way.
In fact, if metaphor is as primordial as it appears to be, there is no other way to philoso-
phize.

I term this a 'temporary resting place" not
only because I hope others will pick up the trail
and follow it further -- if only to deny that I
have been on the right track -- but also because
I suspect that I myself will continue to tussle
with these issues for some time to come. If,
however, I am right about metaphor, then such
future tussles will nevertheless take place
within the metaphoric mode and not outside it.

229

Notes

Chapter Nine

1. <u>Philosophical</u> <u>Investigations</u>, nos. 114-116

2. This is not the place to launch into a full
   epistemological analysis. I have attempted
   to establish the basis for the view adumbrated above in the following writings:
   <u>The</u> <u>Possibility</u> <u>of</u> <u>Religious</u> <u>Knowledge</u>
   (Grand Rapids: Eerdmans, 1971)); "On Reaching
   Bedrock", <u>Metaphilosophy</u>, Oct. 1974; "Saying
   and Showing", <u>Religious</u> <u>Studies</u>, Fall 1974;
   "linguistic Phenomenology" International
   Philosophical Quarterly, and "On Seeing
   Through A Glass, Darkly", Christian Scholars
   Review, May, 1978.

3. <u>Paradox</u> <u>and</u> <u>Discovery</u>, (Oxford:  Blackwells
   1965), p.7

4. <u>Ibid</u>., pp. 3-4.

5. <u>Ibid</u>., p. 132.

6. <u>Ibid</u>., p. 101.

7. <u>Ibid</u>., p. 124.

8. <u>Experience</u> <u>and</u> <u>The</u> <u>Analytic</u> (Chicago:  Univ.
   of Chicago Press, 1958), p. 84

9. <u>Ibid</u>., p. 202.

10. "The Root Metaphor Theory of Metaphysics",
    <u>Journal</u> <u>of</u> <u>Philosophy</u>, Vol. 32 (1935) and
    <u>World</u> <u>Hypotheses</u> (Berkeley:  Univ. of Calif.
    Press. 1942).

11. The Nature of Metaphysical Thinking (London: Macmillan, 1945).

12. The Structure of Scientific Revolutions (2nd. Rd.; Chicago: Univ. of Chicago Press, 1970), p. 10.

13. Ibid., p. 24.

14. Ibid., p. 170.

15. Ibid., p. 103.

16. Ibid., p. 111.

17. Ibid., pp. 204-204.

18. Barry Stroud, "Wittgenstein and Logical Necessity:, Philosophical Review, Oct. 1965, pp. 516-518.